The Enchanting Adventures of Christian Nature

James A. Rousseau Jr.

Edited by Gary T. Dromi, Ph.D.

Copyright © 2022 by James A. Rousseau Jr.

ISBN 978-1-64133-833-2 (softcover)
ISBN 978-1-64133-834-9 (ebook)

All rights reserved. No part of this book may be reproduced or transmitted in any form or by any means, electronic or mechanical, including photocopying, recording, or by any information storage and retrieval system without express written permission from the author, except in the case of brief quotations embodied in critical reviews and certain other noncommercial uses permitted by copyright law.

This book is a work of fiction. Names, characters, places, and incidents are the product of the author's imagination or are used fictitiously. Any resemblance to actual locales, events, or persons, living or dead, is purely coincidental.

Printed in the United States of America.

Brilliant Books Literary
137 Forest Park Lane Thomasville
North Carolina 27360 USA

Contents

Foreword 5
Introduction 7

Part One: Nobody Embraces Patience

Chapter One: The Lesson from a Tree and a Bird 17
Chapter Two: The Lesson from a New Heart 22
Chapter Three: The Lesson from the Illuminating Stars 25
Chapter Four: The Awakening 27
Chapter Five: The Story of Patience 34
Chapter Six: The Journey 40

Part Two: Nobody Learns His Lessons

Chapter One: Nobody Contemplates Who He Is 47
Chapter Two: Nobody Begins to Learn 51
Chapter Three: The Lesson from Mistakes 54
Chapter Four: The Lesson of Being Thankful and Grateful 57
Chapter Five: The Lesson from Forgiveness 60
Chapter Six: The Lesson from Habits 63

Chapter Seven: The Lesson from Anger.. 66
Chapter Eight: The Lesson from Kindness... 69
Chapter Nine: The Lesson of Happiness.. 73

Part Three: Somebody Learns His Lesson

Chapter One: The Identity of Time... 79
Chapter Two: Journey to a Darkened Heart.. 85
Chapter Three: Time and Christian Nature Meet Somebody.............. 88
Chapter Four: The Repentance of Somebody.. 96
Chapter Five: Stephan's New Heart.. 100
Chapter Six: Stephan's Camp Meeting with God 105
Chapter Seven: Stephan's New Identity and Adventure.................... 109

Part Four: Life in the Enchanted Land

Chapter One: The God-Centered Nature Filled Heart 117
Chapter Two: The God-Centered Christian Nature Filled Heart........... 120
Chapter Three: The Royal Adventure of King Time and
    Queen Christian Nature 125
Chapter Four: The Homecoming of Saint Nicholaus....................... 130
Chapter Five: The Royal Wedding 135

Conclusion 143

Foreword

The Enchanting Adventures of Christian Nature is a wonderful, fictional, love story, a story about courage, friendship, love, and God's grace. But it's more than just a story. There are deep Biblical truths woven throughout every chapter: forgiveness, kindness, patience, love, and grace.

As a writer, Mr. Rousseau, has exercised his artistic license to tell a story about God's love, grace and forgiveness for those who believe and receive Christ as their Savior. He has also written in such a way as to cause the readers to reflect upon their own lives and how they are living them.

Mr. Rousseau writes like an artist paints, with great depth and feeling. Instead of using paints to bring out the depth of the story and the characters on a canvas, he uses words on a page, descriptive words that allow the readers' imaginations to construct each character and scene for themselves.

It is an honor and a privilege to be asked to edit Mr. Rousseau's first book. He is a man with a big smile, a kind heart and, always, an encouraging word for those around him. His love for the Lord and His amazing grace is contagious.

It is my hope and prayer that you, dear reader, will immerse yourself in this literary journey, mine the gold nuggets of biblical truths and find great joy in this journey of the heart.

By His Grace,
Gary T. Dromi, Ph.D.

Introduction

Imagine living in a God-created heart in the world of your imagination. Imagine living in a world where the Holy Spirit lovingly and tenderly fills every nook and cranny of your heart with the beauty of Christian Nature. Imagine living in a world where goodness, kindness, love, gentleness, peace, and joy, like delicious fruits, beckons you to partake of their sweet taste from each Holy Spirit-filled assorted tree that you become acquainted with. Imagine living in a world where each citizen, like a cherished and highly valued goblet, is filled to overflowing with enchanted golden drops of comfort to freely pour upon everyone whom their lives may touch. Imagine living in a world where the only purpose of each citizen is to live to bring glory to God and be a comfort and a source of encouragement to all whom they meet in their own personal adventure through life. Imagine living in a world where each citizen places their cup filled with goodness to the parched, dry lips of the weary traveler, who has not tasted the refreshing acts of goodness for a long time. And in so doing, restoring life to that previously hardened person who was on the verge of losing his life to a thirst for goodness in a hardened world.

Is this the kind of world in which you would like to live? "Sounds nice," you may say, "but this is not real life!" The purpose of this literary endeavor, the reason for this story, is to reveal to each beloved reader that this world is real. It really does exist! It exists in our own God-created heart, and the Holy Spirit, who has filled it with the beauty of Christian Nature, lovingly invites you to live here as a cherished citizen, all the days of the enchanted adventure of your life! Please accept this specially addressed invitation just for you, for it has your very own name on it. Please come into this world, the world of Nathanael Nobody. For you see, my friend, Nathanael stands at the door leading into this world. He is slowly opening the door just for you! With a warm and gentle smile he tenderly embraces you, and with tears of joy in his eyes he welcomes you into a new world of kindness and goodness that some may never see. This world, which really does exist, has a special place just for you! A hand-woven welcome mat has been lovingly placed right before your feet. If you will but enter through the door that Nathanael is opening for you, there you will find a world made up of citizens wearing smiles so large that their faces can hardly contain them! For you see, my precious friend, they are inviting you into their world, your potential world! Will you enter, my dear friend? Do you want to enter? Do you think it is a dream, or could it possibly be real? The invitation is just for you, and you alone, if you will only take it!

This world is real and it has the potential to exist in the enchanted land of your own heart. It can only be seen with the deep penetrating eyes of your own understanding heart. The sweet, nurturing words of its citizens can only be heard with the ears of a precisely tuned-in heart. The realness of this world can only be felt as the hands of the heart desperately reach out to touch the kindness, gentleness, goodness, and genuine love that each citizen earnestly desires to give you as a free gift!

Some may laugh at such a world and say that it could not possibly exist. For at this point in their lives, all they know is a world of vanity, greed, selfishness, envy, criticism, lust, and all sorts of evil speaking. That world would be a horrible place to live in. If you were given a choice to continue living your life in such a world, or leaving that world and living in a new world of love, goodness, and kindness, would you? Would you make that choice?

Again, you may say that such a world does not exist. Nathanael Nobody's answer would be, "Why not?" Why not let God create His own world within the heart of your imagination? Why not let the Holy Spirit, through Patience, fill it with the beauty of Christian Nature, making it real, bringing it out in this world and inviting others to live in this world also? If we would each choose to let God create within our heart, a world filled by the Holy Spirit with kindness and a love for others, the world that we choose to live in, we will find that we are not alone. There are many others who have devoted themselves to living in the world of their God-created heart, and have chosen to be a blessing to all whom their lives may touch. My precious friend, again, this is the sole purpose – the reason for this story – that you may see the importance of living your life in this God-created world of your heart, under the influence of the Holy Spirit, to encourage others to come to God and live in this wonderful world also. All of this for the purpose of truly bringing glory to God and being a source of encouragement to all whom our lives may touch.

Yes, my dear friend, this world is very real! A truly enchanted adventure awaits you, if you are genuinely willing to look with the eyes of your longing heart to see such a land of absolute beauty. Our external eyes are incapable of seeing such a land. Our external eyes can only see what their external hands can touch and their external ears can hear. A seemingly magical adventure awaits you, if you will allow the Holy Spirit of God to teach you the skill of seeing, hearing, and feeling with the eyes, ears, and hands of your heart!

O my dear friend, my precious friend, you who my external eyes may never see but my heart's eyes see so ever-lovingly. My heart leaps with joy for you to enter this world that is real, that has the potential to exist within your own heart, and which will enable you to be a source of comfort and encouragement to all whom your life may touch as your adventure takes you through your forest of life. Could it be that this story is not about Nathanael and Patience, but it is about you and the Holy Spirit, as the Holy Spirit, through Patience, seeks to fill every part of your God-created heart with the beauty of Christian Nature? Remember this world can only be seen when one begins to look with the eyes of one's heart. This is a world where the comforting, loving, kind sounds of other like-minded citizens can only be heard with the ears of one's heart!

Once again, you may ask, "Is such a place – to spend the remaining days of my life – really possible?" This writer believes it is! This writer believes that as he writes the words of this page, it is not his hand that is writing, but his heart! It is my heart listening intently to your heart telling me that, "yes" this is the world you would really like to live in, if at all possible! So you see, this is not a story from my hand. This is a story about you, conveying through my heart, the world that you would really like to live in, isn't it?

We must remember that, regretfully, many will always deny that such a world exists. "It's only a fantasy, an illusion, your imagination," they will say. Many will seek to destroy this enchanted land of your dreams. Deep inside your God-created heart you know that it really does exist, and has been filled by the Holy Spirit who has been patiently waiting for you to live here for a very long time.

This writer encourages you to put yourself into the very shoes of Nathanael Nobody. Please do not be an outsider, one who would just pick this book up and read it casually as you would read any other. For deep inside your heart, you know that you are Nathanael, longing for such an incredible adventure. Deep inside your own heart you long to see these true-to-life adventures that you know to be true. You long to quietly ponder the beauty of the giant redwoods as the soft, cool, breeze of Christian Nature, herself, tenderly caresses your face with enchanted kisses of Christian natural sweetness. You long to listen to the sweet tunes coming forth from Christian Nature, as the loving sounds coming from cheerful birds puts a smile on your face and consumes your heart with joy. You long to put one foot in front of another and personally experience the events of life. You long to quietly meditate and listen to the musical talent of the melodious melody of a refreshing stream, like the living water coming from God Himself harmonizes wonderfully with the natural talent of the singing rocks. In the same way, the Holy Spirit seeks to beautifully harmonize your life with Christian Nature. Your old heart crawls through the dry desert of life with thirst. With parched and cracked lips you come to this life-giving stream of cool, refreshing water bubbling forth from your new heart. You drink from this truly magical goblet, filled to overflowing with golden drops of life-enhancing comfort. You long to tenderly walk through this enchanted world of Queen Christian Nature herself, enjoying, with your new heart's eyes, all that she has to show you. You long to meet new people in this new-enchanted land of your heart. They invite you to drink from their cups of wonder of what life would be like if each person was consumed with a heart filled to overflowing with love, kindness, gentleness, and a desire to be a real comfort to everyone whom their lives may touch.

So you see, my very precious friend, this is not a story written by some distant person who is a stranger to you. This is a story about you, about me, about all persons who desire to live in a freshly created world of a new heart, one filled with all the joys of our imagination! A heart that we can bring out and live in this temporary world of our temporal body. And maybe, just maybe, make life in this other world more enjoyable to all whom our lives may touch.

This storyteller, your storyteller, feels from his new heart that you will be my cherished friend forever! For if you will begin to look with the eyes of your heart, you will see this magical and enchanted world that truly is real, if, you will but look at all things with the eyes of your God-created heart. It will be my privilege to shake your hand, give you a big hug, and with tears flowing down the cheeks of my face, I will welcome you into this wonderful land that is real, but exists only in our hearts!

My heart-felt cherished forever-friend, please remember that you will never travel in this world of enchantment alone. A very special love of your heart, the Holy Spirit, seen in the beauty of Patience, will patiently love you, guide you, open your heart's eyes, comfort you, and teach you all that she knows. She will lovingly, and through Patience, reveal to you the ways of Christian Nature herself. Yes, Queen Christian Nature herself will patiently teach you the worth and value of the intangible gifts that God has given to her to lovingly share with you. So always remember that the soft, loving hand of the Holy Spirit, in the form of the beautiful Patience, will always be with you, holding your hand and guiding you through this vast forest of life itself.

As you walk hand-in-hand in this world of your new heart, with the love of your new heart, and Patience tenderly guiding you, you will meet many never before seen people. You will find that you become a new person. All the experiences of your previous life will mysteriously, and magically be brought together. And the enchanted wisdom of Time will be freely given to you as a gift from God to freely give to others.

O my very dear friend, could it really be that you are the true Nathanael Nobody and I am nothing more than an insignificant Nobody? Would you please give me the privilege of letting our new hearts beat together as one? For what we see, hear, and feel in our real life can never be seen, heard, or felt with our external eyes, ears, and hands. It can only be seen, heard, and felt with the reality that exists in our hearts; for this is where we all truly live!

So now, as a doorman would gently bow to one desiring to enter a beloved dwelling, so this undeserving Nobody lovingly bows to you; and with a smile on my face as large as a dinner plate, and with tears of everlasting joy streaming down my face, I beckon you, as a forever-to-be-cherished friend, to enter the real world of Nathanael Nobody. May you be him, making his world your world. And as you go through this door, may it take you through the door of your new heart and fill you with a truly magical and enchanted adventure that can only be experienced in your new heart.

Your Forever Friend!
James A. Rousseau, Jr.

We do not look at the things which are seen, but at the things which are not seen. For the things which are seen are temporary, but the things which are not seen are eternal.

2 Corinthians 4:18

Part One

Nobody Embraces Patience

Chapter One

The Lesson from a Tree and a Bird

An enchanted, soft and gentle kiss from the lips of one with tender hands, ever so lovingly caressed every inch of Nathanael Nobody's time-expired face. The uniqueness of this sweet honey-anointed kiss brings with it the precious treasure of a fresh excitement, such as a young child would experience on their very first Christmas morning. The freshness of this new sensation seemed to saturate every cell of his beleaguered body. "What a truly magical kiss this is!" he thought. "Coming from the lips of one whom I cannot see, touched by hands which I can only feel, and mysteriously disguised by the breath of fresh air against my face."

In this seemingly new and completely exhilarated state, Nobody carefully ponders his thoughts as he consciously considers each delicate step he takes through nature's forest of life itself. With his heart leading him on this newly discovered adventure, he finds his focus drawn to one of many giant redwood trees. As a highly skilled artist would carefully place his particular object of interest on the very landscape of his canvas, so the artistic ability of the master artist is freely made available for all to see on the canvas of this beautiful forest. What Nobody sees is a true masterpiece! He studies the bark of this massive work of art. Each detail of the rugged bark giving evidence to the fact that it sacrifices its own personal welfare to provide protection from the storms of life to the trunk of the tree itself. The mighty trunk, so huge in its all-encompassing circumference, slowly reaches skyward as if pointing to its creator. Each branch filled with not only a beauty pleasing to the eyes, but also teeming with many families of animal life which look to this tree as their home, and depend on it to provide for their daily needs. He notices on the ground a very small seed, which he proceeds to investigate. He begins to understand that this majestic provider didn't start as a giant in this forest of life, but it started as a small seed. It took much time and enduring patience through the many storms of life for that little seed to grow into a beautiful mature tree. Through this newfound understanding he came to realize that the primary purpose of maturity, as seen in this fully mature masterpiece, is to live for the purpose of bringing enjoyment and providing for the needs of all whom its life may touch.

Once again he felt the soft, gentle kiss anointed with the fruit of the honeybees. Only this time the kiss was skillfully placed directly on his lips. He could feel the warmness of delicate hands treasuring his cheeks as if they were of great value. He could not help but feel a pure intoxication coming over him as these sweet hands gave forth a natural scent of the purity of true love. He could sense a feeling of eyes to his eyes, nose to his nose, reading and studying his eyes as if unveiling his very soul. "Who is this fascinating being who is so passionately embracing me?" he thought. "Indeed, this is truly an enchanted place!"

In the quietness of the moment, it was then that Nobody heard a still small voice say "Look up my Nathanael, look up in the tree." He looked up and directed the entire focus of his attention to a very small, seemingly insignificant bird that gave every indication of being consumed with a spirit of happiness and joy. As he gazed in wonder and great delight at the inspirational little creature, he could hear a sweet tune that proceeded from the very soul of this enchanted bird. This sweet melody nourished his soul in much the same way that the life enhancing nectar of a God-provided flower feeds the honeybees. Again, the still small voice whispers into the ears of his heart a story, which will consume him all the days of his life. This one, whom Nobody could not see, placed her precious hands, which felt as soft and tender as newly spun silk, on his and whispered this story into his ears:

"There were once three birds. One bird appeared to be consumed with a personal vanity and a love for itself. Known by many as a "peacock," this near-sighted manifestation of pride would strut around all day and do whatever possible to get the attention of others. Fully absorbed with displaying its own pretended beauty to others, this peacock proved disgusting to all whom its life touched. Its feathers, when first looked at, gave the illusion of beauty. But when examined more closely, revealed a bird that only pretended to be attractive to others. In reality, it was poor in regard to being a comfort or source of encouragement to others. This bird had poor flying ability. It could barely lift itself off the ground and be a part of the beauty that the heavens above could have offered it. Each disgusting sound from its mouth seemed to utter that it was the only important bird and that no other bird really mattered.

The second bird, known to many as a "crow," was given the ability to fly higher than the proud peacock. Even though it was given this ability to fly higher so that it could see the needs of others and be a real source of encouragement to them, it chose not to be. Its two wings were named "selfishness" and "covetousness." When it would see another bird, its only thought was to take advantage of that bird for its own personal gain. It would always be greedy for more and more, and never feel that it had enough. The irritating sound that came from its heart was filled with faultfinding and the belittling of all other birds. Whenever it would appear, all the birds would flee because they feared that what they had would be taken away from them.

The third bird is this precious little inspirational bird, which you have been gazing at. It has the ability to fly higher than all other birds and because of this it can see farther than any other bird. It sees and feels from it's little heart, all the vanity, selfishness, and greed which consumes so many birds. It has two wings: one called "goodness" the other called "kindness." It lives solely for the selfless purpose of spreading goodness and kindness to all whom its life may touch. Its exquisite external beauty is a mirror image of its internal heart. As other birds see this beautiful touch of true happiness in this joyous bird, they flock to it for the goodness, kindness, and selfless acts of love that this remarkable bird encourages and comforts their hearts with."

The storyteller now placed those tender, delicate unseen hands on his timeworn face and said, "You have a choice to make, my precious Nathanael. Which bird will you be? A proud, vain bird who only desires to draw attention to itself and it's own fake beauty? A depressing bird that is controlled by selfishness and greed, and only sees others as nothing more than objects from which it can take something? Or will you choose to be a comforting and encouraging bird, who's every flight is energized by goodness and kindness, and who's every tune, springing forth from its soul, is consumed with bringing happiness and joy to the hearing ear of all whom its life may touch?" At this, Nobody could feel a very intense presence of this sweet one whom he could not see. He could feel these words of truth penetrate the very heart of his soul, as an arrow would penetrate from the bow of a highly skilled archer.

Nobody stood looking up into the tree, studying this beautiful little inspirational bird. He couldn't help but realize what wonderful creations of God that both this little bird and majestic tree are. "What amazing lessons they have taught me this day," he thought. "It seems that they both have a life's purpose of bringing comfort and encouragement to all whom their lives may touch." As Nobody resumed his thoughtful walk through this enchanted forest of life, he came to understand more fully the value of the true treasure that this tree and bird had given to him as a gift this day.

He couldn't help but wonder how it was possible, that through all the years of his life he would walk through this forest many times, and yet, just walk right by them without ever having eyes to see them as they really are. He fully tasted these newfound treasures, which seemed so sweet to the taste buds of one who had lost the ability to taste such treats. Nobody, in a moment of intense and passionate crying, cries out to God to please open the eyes of his heart and send someone to open the eyes of his understanding, so that he might be able to see clearly those truths which are internally true, but which he had never seen before.

At this moment, he could definitely feel two arms tenderly wrapping themselves around his body. He could feel a delicate head against his chest. He could mysteriously feel dampness on his chest, as if someone were shedding a loving stream of tears on his very heart. A still small voice he could hear whispering, "I love you, my heart's desire, my beloved, and I will never ever leave you!" At that moment he thought, "Who is this truly enchanted precious woman who has so captured the very soul of my existence?"

"Oh God," he cries out, "I must see this remarkable sweet love of my soul! I must be given eyes to see this woman who has captivated the love of my heart." The voice whispers, "Be patient my dear Nathanael, be patient my true love; for in time you will see!" "What a wonderful place of enchantment this is," he thought. "O God, please give me these eyes to see what and who I have never seen before." The voice whispers, "My dear one, do you really know what you are asking for? What you ask is extremely difficult to achieve and yet simple to attain." Nathanael cries out, "Oh how I wish to see you! This one who I can feel so tenderly and who I already treasure dearly, though I cannot see you!" She whispers, "In time my dear Nathanael, in time. First, however, there are many new things for you to see in your new heart."

Chapter Two

The Lesson from a New Heart

From deep within the being of Nathanael Nobody a very strange occurrence takes place. From out of the depths of his soul a refreshing, bubbling fountain of life-giving water begins to flow. His thirsty old heart begins to drink deeply of this magical fountain that he has discovered for the very first time. As he drinks and drinks and drinks some more, he finds his skin becoming younger, his strength and stamina become stronger, and all signs of old age seem to disappear as if they had never been. "How can this be," he thought? "I have actually found the so-called fountain of youth! Could it be that the fountain of youth and the so-called Shangri-La actually do exist? Throughout the history of the ages there have been many people who have searched for these fabled places, but lo and behold, they really do exist. They exist in our own hearts!"

A newfound exhilaration from this land of true enchantment seemed to lift Nobody up and out of one world and into another. This new and totally unexplainable youth encouraged him to run and jump and play. In the midst of all of this excitement, a new discovery was about to be found. He could hear the natural melodious symphony of a nearby stream of water harmonizing with the musical expertise of the singing rocks. He instantly found himself becoming an admiring guest of this orchestra of natural talent. As all of his senses were enjoying the symphony, a unique never before seen delicacy at the streams edge got his attention. As he plucked it from the stream, he became fascinated by it. It looked like some unknown fruit. It was similar to an orange, yet it was shaped like a pear. He bit deeply into it and found his mouth full of the taste of a honeycomb. This sweet moist taste of heavenly delight seemed to open a set of brand new eyes, filled with wonder and a craving to discover new things, such as a new-born baby would have upon opening their eyes for the first time. His seemingly just-created heart's eyes were now seeing all things in a way he had never seen before. Yes, indeed, my dear reader, for the first time ever, Nathanael Nobody could now see and feel what he had never seen or felt before. He began to realize that all his life, when he looked at something, he only saw what others were manipulating him to see. When he listened to others, he only heard what others wanted him to hear. Now, though, this brand new heart seemed to briskly and loudly beat like a skilled drummer! He could now, for the very first time, see and hear and feel clearly all that had been totally invisible to him before.

This newness of discovery enabled him to see a freshness in everything that he had not seen before. There was, now, nothing old. Everything became like new to him. As he pondered these new events happening to him, he found the sight of his new heart directing its attention into his very own mind. Like an explorer filled with the excitement of discovering a new land for the first time, he discovered that there is a vast expanse of his mind, which had never been touched by his new heart's eyes before.

With this newfound zeal, vision, and feeling, he ran and jumped and played without ever getting tired. "What a wonderful thing has happened to me!" he cries out. At this moment he could hear a girlish child-like giggle behind him filled with happiness over his happiness. "O my dear one," cries the voice. "Truly you are happy because you can now see wonderful, never-before-seen gifts in everyday places where, before, you didn't see anything. O my love, it is God who has now given you a new heart to see and feel what others may never see or feel. Feel me with your heart, my forever love, not with your hands. See me with your heart. For only when you see me with your heart will you see me for the first time!"

With a greatly excited heart, Nobody heard these words from the lips of one who, by now, has become beloved by him. He falls to his knees and cries out to God in prayer, "Thank you, O God, for opening my eyes and for the first time showing me the best and most beautiful treasures that any eyes can see. Thank you, O God for the renewal of youth and for the happiness you have brought to this unworthy being."

Once again a feeling of extreme intimate closeness engulfed him, as if a body had just wrapped herself around him; and once again tears of joy moistened his chest as the sweet voice says, "O my love, my precious one, how I have waited so long for you. How I love you! Never, ever, will I leave you. I am forever yours and you are forever mine!" "O God," Nobody cries out, "Thank you so very much for helping me to see what I have never seen before. But when, O God, will I see this one who loves such an unworthy creature as myself? Please, O God, I must see her. Please! Please! Please!" "Soon, my love," the voice whispers. "Very soon!"

Chapter Three

The Lesson from the Illuminating Stars

"What a remarkable day this has been," thought Nathanael as he rehearsed what his new heart had taught his freshly discovered mind on this forever-to-be-remembered day. By now this amazing day had transformed itself into the beauty of the night. It was at this eternal moment, in the enchanted life of Nathanael Nobody, that he could feel the warmness of a soft delicate hand take his hand and lead him under a naturally sculpted redwood masterpiece. As he could strangely feel the very pulse in this warm hand, he heard these sweet words, "Come sit with me." As Nathanael placed his body under the tree he could feel the warmth of another body cuddle up next to him and snuggle her head and heart over his own. Then it happened! Nathanael knew that he was not alone! Over his heart he could very definitely feel two hearts beating! His chest became wet with tears. A soft delicate warmness of some still unseen woman had snuggled up to him and placed her heart over his own: two hearts beating! He thought, "This cannot be my imagination. This is real!" Then that tender delicate hand lifted his own and pointed his finger to the beautiful stars in the quiet sky. Then that sweet voice, coming from the lips of the one whom he still could not see, asked him a question, "My love, if people in the other world would look at the stars at night, do you think they would live their lives in a different way? God tells us if we would consider his heavens, the work of his fingers, the moon and the stars, we would look at ourselves and say, 'O God why do you even think about me?' For you see, my true love, the heavens truly do show us God's glory and the work of his hands (Psalms 8, 19). Each day God speaks to our hearts; each day He reveals His knowledge to our hearts. O my darling and most precious Nathanael, can you understand that your physical eyes, your physical ears, your physical hands are only designed for temporal use as we walk with our eyes and ears open in the other world? To see what is truly real we must master the skill of seeing, hearing, and feeling with our heart. It is only when we gain this keenness of sight, hearing, and feeling that we begin to see what is truly real! So my love, what does your heart see when you look at the stars?" "O my precious one," cries Nathanael, feeling her heart beating now with his own heart, as one heart. "I see eternity and my insignificance in it!" Immediately he could feel two tender, soft, warm delicate hands on each of his cheeks. He could very clearly feel a rapid succession of tear-induced, true-love-inspired kisses all over his face, followed by two arms wrapping around his neck, and the sweetest lips ever known to man, pressed, as if eternally, against his lips. These lips whispered, "O my darling, how I so love you. My very heart is your heart! We are one being now and forever!"

As Nathanael and his sweetheart held each other closely and looked at the stars together, the eyesight of Nathanael's heart was beginning to focus; it was becoming keener and keener. He could now see with his new heart much more clearly; he could now hear with his new ears much more clearly; and truly feel with his heart what is real. He began to think how very sad it was, that so few people really do see the things in the heavens and in the earth with the eyes of their heart. "O God," Nathanael cries out, "I will praise You for I am fearfully and wonderfully made. Marvelous are your works and I know that to be true!" (Psalm 139). As face was against face, Nathanael could feel her soft hand sweetly stroke his hair. As they both looked up together into the quiet beautiful starry sky, Nathanael's eyes grew heavy and as he went to sleep, the sweetheart of his life covered him with a blanket saturated with kisses. Looking into his now sleeping eyes, this sweetest of all creations whispered, "Sleep my love for tomorrow you will see me clearly as I am!"

Chapter Four

The Awakening

As the skillful precision of a doctor would carefully remove a cataract from the eye of a patient, so the Master physician slowly and methodically removed every trace of old cataracts that previously had blinded the eyes of Nathanael Nobody's heart. Yes, my dear reader, as this momentous day dawns and the eyelids in Nathanael's head slowly open, the great awakening of Nathanael Nobody begins. This is a strange day, indeed, for he awoke with an absolutely perfect heart-vision. The very first thing he heard on this perfect day was the singing of his little special inspirational bird. He was tempted to let his heart sing with the bird, but instead he just smiled and drank deeply from the goblet filled to overflowing with the beauty of the moment. He began to realize, that with each moment of this enchanted life that each one of us lives, there is a special gift of the experience gained from all other moments, that is given as a treasure-chest filled with valuable riches of wisdom to enhance the value of each upcoming moment. An all-consuming feeling of joyful glee seemed to course through every cell of his existence as he thought, "So this is what it means to fully enjoy life!"

All of sudden he could see, with his heart, numerous people, all happy and in joyous spirits, calling out to him, "Time has come to arise and seek adventure!" Many people were running up close to him, yet stopping short. They were intently looking at every detail of his face and studying his every feature, as if he were someone of great importance. They were carefully putting their hands over their mouths and were whispering something to each other. What were they saying? He knew they were talking about him, but what were they whispering to each other? There were still many things that he had no knowledge or understanding of. Each day continued to bring with it a basket of new, never-before-known findings that continue to amaze his newly enlightened heart. He had discovered the riches of silence, that if he would just sit quietly at the feet of his own life, and let the experiences of his own life teach him, that what he learned would greatly enhance the seeing, hearing, and feeling skills of his own heart. Nathanael chose to listen intently to their whispers. What he heard greatly confused him. They said, "Time has come. Time has finally arrived. Christian Nature must be so very filled with happiness because her special Time has finally arrived." "What is all this about 'Time' and 'Christian Nature,'" he thought? "I do not understand what this means. They all talk about 'Time' and 'Christian Nature' as if they were people, while they stare at me as if I were some important person."

"This is all so very strange to me," he thought. "Before I could see from my heart I would walk through this very forest of life and I never once saw anyone. But now I see all these people who seem to know me." From amongst this vast crowd of people a man named Ahira Naphtali came up to Nathanael, placed one hand on Nathanael's shoulder and placed his right hand in Nathanael's and said, "Welcome, my king into the real world of reality where sight, sound, and feel all come from the heart!" With this Nathanael spoke up and introduced himself as "Nobody." "My name is Nobody, Nathanael Nobody." Simultaneous laughter broke out amongst the crowd. He could hear them saying to each other, "He calls himself 'Nobody.' Does he not have any idea who he really is? Maybe the middle name of Patience that God has given to Christian Nature is fitting, for she has shown a lot of patience in not revealing to him who he really is up to this point."

As they whispered these words to each other, he became stunned with confusion as to what all of this meant. The one who had always explained these strange things to him was nowhere to be found! Then he became consumed with a deep sorrow of heart, for in the midst of all of these wonderful never-before-seen people he felt completely alone. A crushing, devastating, all consuming depression engulfed his entire being. For the one with the sweet honey-anointed kiss, hands as soft as newly spun silk, who lovingly caressed every inch of his time-worn face, who placed her heart over his as their two hearts became one, and promised to never leave him, was nowhere to be found! This overwhelming weight of aloneness absolutely crushed him! He dropped to his knees and, in the sight of all, began crying great rivers of sorrow made up of the tears of his broken heart!

As he is consumed with weeping, the crowd gathers around Ahira Naphtali and confers with him. They say, "Ahira, you must tell him who he really is. He must know the truth!" To this Ahira raises an index finger to them and says, "Hush! This is not for us to do. Queen Christian Nature, in her time, will reveal these things to him. Well did God give her the name of Patience, for she is truly patient in all she teaches! What we will do, though, is encourage this one who calls himself 'Nobody,' for he will soon be our king. We will let our Queen, Christian Nature, patiently teach him and bring him along as he slowly comes to understand who he really is. There is to be no more laughing at him. Remember, you would be laughing at our king. If Queen Christian Nature heard of this, she would not be happy with us at all! So we will encourage our king and let Queen Christian Nature take care of all other things."

As the crowd gathered back around the sobbing, down on his knees Nobody, they found someone totally consumed and broken with the grief of his aloneness. He cries out, "I must put an end to my life and be done with living, for I have no desire to live without my sweetheart! I cannot live and do not want to live without her!" The crowd shouts to Ahira, "Do something Ahira! You must not allow Time to be killed! It would severely injure all of eternity! Do something!" At this Ahira drops to his knees beside the uncontrollable Nathanael Nobody and puts a loving arm around the shoulders of his weeping, broken, soon-to-be king. "She is not gone, my king, or as you call yourself, 'Nobody.' She is not gone at all. Our beloved queen has merely gone, temporarily, to prepare herself for you to see her for the first time. O yes, and who is it that you call yourself again?" "I am Nobody; just a very insignificant

Nathanael Nobody. Why do you keep calling me your king? I am no king. I am Nobody! The love of my heart – you call her your queen – she is my sweetheart! She belongs to me and me alone! I am forever hers and she is forever mine! You say she is not gone. If I am truly your king, as you say, then I command to see her now! O how I understand none of this. All of this is just so confusing to me."

A stunned silence then fell over the crowd. Ahira says, "Listen everyone, she is coming; our queen is coming quickly!" From deep within the forest of life, an exceptionally strong wind begins to blow. Everyone can hear as the wind blows through the giant redwoods, the comforting, nurturing words that go directly into Nathanael's heart. They magically whisper, "Nathanael, Nathanael, my heart's love. I come to you! How I love you! I come!" From deep within the woods, it is amazing what everyone sees. The clean, cool, fresh wind seems to be carefully parting the trees, as if someone was briskly coming towards them. A scent of sweetness permeated the air with a sort of intoxication, which seemed to cast a spell of excitement upon all.

"Rise my king! Rise!" Ahira says to Nathanael. "It won't be long before she's here!" Ahira gently wipes away the tears from Nathanael's face. Others come up, one by one, and also wipe tears from the face of Nathanael Nobody. They each kiss his hands. One by one they give him big hugs and in unison they say, "We have been waiting for you for a long time!" All of these words are so confusing to Nathanael who, up until a couple of days ago, had spent all his life living in a different world, a world of vanity, greed, selfishness, envy, violence, and evil-speaking. Now, all of this is just absolutely amazing! "How can this be? Why could I not see you all before?" Ahira tells him, "Because you would not see, hear, or feel with your heart." Ahira then spoke for all by saying, "Never forget, 'Nobody,' as you call yourself, that external eyes, ears, and hands are designed and given to us by God only as motor skills that we may walk, hear, and see in the other world. But in the truly real world, where God is the King of kings, where we choose to live, sight, sound, and feel come only from our new hearts."

As Ahira Naphtali spoke to Nathanael, the crowd behind Ahira and in front of Nathanael took a huge collective gasp, bowed a knee and their head toward the ground. As this exceptionally large crowd then rose to their feet, the women put their hands over their mouths and were sobbing great tears of joy. The men, with arms folded, were smiling so large that the smile covered their whole face. For all of these wonderful people were fully aware that their Queen, Christian Nature, the perfect, pure true love of Nathanael Nobody's heart, had arrived and was silently standing about twenty feet behind him.

Ahira looked into the face of the bewildered Nathanael, who was wondering what it was that immediately brought about the change in the people. With a smile that could not be suppressed Ahira said, "Our king, are you ready to see, with your heart's eyes, our queen, the love of your heart's desire?" Then the vast crowd all in unison said, "Turn around, our king, and look!" With his heart beating so fast that he knew his chest could not contain it, he turned and looked and saw with his heart, for the first time, the most beautiful human female ever sculpted by the supernatural hands of her Divine Creator! Standing nearly six feet tall, her head was covered with extremely thick, deep rich auburn hair that cascaded down to her waist and flowed freely down her front and back. The treasure of this extraordinary beauty that Nathanael was beholding reminded him of a waterfall, mysteriously veiling a face behind the refreshing waters. Parted down the middle, her deep thick auburn hair was defined by a braided crown of her hair surrounding the circumference of the top of the head of this divine creation of Nathanael's love. Her skin was creamy white, as if no form of defilement had ever touched her. She wore a one-piece gown of pure white silk, specially spun for her on this special day by her friends the caterpillars. Her head was bowed low and her precious face was fully veiled from Nathanael's sight by her cascading hair.

Nathanael could hear her sobbing with tears freely flowing down her pure white silk gown. Ahira whispered into Nathanael's ears, "Her name is 'Patience', my king. Her name is 'Patience,' for she has been waiting for you and just for you only for a very, very long time!" With a trembling voice Nathanael calls, "Patience." She slowly raises her head and as her auburn hair slowly unveils her face for Nathanael to see for the very first time, he can see tears streaming down a face of pure milky white beauty! Her deep blue eyes are as if they were skillfully designed from the hands of a master artist. Never before in all of creation has anyone possessed such ocean-blue-eyes as Patience. Looking into her fully unveiled eyes was like looking intently into the blue beauty of gentle sounding ocean waters. It was as if these beautiful blue ocean-water-eyes were revealing for the very first time, the visible soul of the love of Nathanael's heart.

It was at this time that Nathanael heard the familiar voice now speaking words to him, for the first time, from a sobbing face, which he could clearly see. With trembling lips and sobbing eyes, those deep blue-ocean-eyes meekly look into Nathanael's and says, "O my love, my hearts only desire, do you find me pleasing to your sight?"

Nathanael broke into a fast run toward Patience and she towards him. As they met they embraced in such a tender way as had never been seen before by any kind of eyes. They both fell into a complete, total and absolute emotional breakdown. Both were rapidly and uncontrollably kissing every inch of each other's face. They kissed each other's tears away, only to be followed by more tears of pure love and joy. At this point, they were both so consumed with kissing, caressing, and hugging that there was clearly no way possible for the crowd to get the attention of their queen and future king. Finally Nathanael looked into Patience's deep ocean-blue-eyes and said, "Are you really real?" With a smile so big it seemed to encompass the entire world of Christian Nature herself, she nodded her head up and down vigorously. Such a scene was so moving upon the crowd that husbands began kissing their sobbing-with-delight wives, and a scene of happiness and joy filled the hearts of everyone in this beautiful, real world of fulfilled dreams.

"This calls for a time of celebration," calls out Ahira Naphtali. "Bring out the flutes, the mandolins, and the tambourines. Let's all dance and celebrate the day with our king and queen!" As the celebration takes place, Patience, interlocking her arm around Nathanael's, takes him around to each and every person and introduces him to each one, leaving no one out. She personally thanks each one for being a part of their celebration. "So many wonderful people," Nathanael whispers to Patience, "who have always been here but I have never seen before." To this Patience kisses the tip of her index finger, smiles, and gently touches the tip of his nose with the kissed index finger and says, "That's because you were not looking with the eyes of your heart, my precious Nathanael. For all of these people have been here for a long time waiting for us to come together. You had just devoted your life to being so consumed with the demands, cares, and responsibilities of the other world that you could never see any of these people or even me." "O how I love you so very much Patience," says Nathanael. Then, for the first time he actually saw that sweet precious head gently placed over his heart and could feel the loving streams of happy tears moisten his heart. Yes, my dear reader, at this magical moment it would be impossible for Nathanael Nobody to be any happier.

"This day is like a day filled with boxes of gifts that God has given to me," thought Nathanael. "As I untie the ribbons of each gift and open them up, it is as if I find a new treasure in each one." Patience then whispers to Nathanael, "From this point on and forever more, you will find that you will no longer look at time as measured in days or years but rather in moments, with each moment of your existence being a treasure. Not even you, my love, as Time himself, can change the past for anyone. You can only influence others to take the experiences they have learned from the past, and enrich the value of the treasure they now have in the moment."

What a time of great happiness and joy flooded this enchanted world of tall evergreens, as everyone was devoted to bringing kindness to all whom they sang and danced with. Nathanael noticed at this time, that his special little inspirational bird, whom he could hold in the palm of his hand, never left him but perched on his shoulder and stayed with him at all times. He couldn't help but notice Patience wink at the bird and then with a twinkle from her deep blue eyes she said, "By the way, my love, the time has come for you to know that your little bird has a name, its Aeromore! The mightiest and most powerful creation ever made by God and your protector forever!" A totally bewildered Nathanael looked into the palm of his hand and noticed little two-inch Aeromore in his hand, tweeting a tune up to Nathanael's ears. Nathanael's other hand was scratching his own head and he said, "So you are the mighty Aeromore, my protector!" Patience winked to Aeromore who seemed to wink back to her and Nathanael said, "Indeed, for why should I be surprised in this wonderful real world of enchantment!"

With laughter, joy, and excitement saturating the very existence of all, each one realizing that God had given them all the power to make everyday a path of flowers, Ahira Naphtali steps forward to share with the people a story that will become a legend in the history books of all who live in the God-created heart of their own imaginations.

Chapter Five

The Story of Patience

"Once upon a time, when God told Adam and Eve to leave the Garden of Eden, a child was born to this first man and woman. This was the very first baby born in the world. This little baby was named 'Evangeline.' She was named such by her mother Eve that she would devote her life to spreading the good news of God's love and share the beauty of goodness and kindness to all whom her life may touch. This was truly the love of her mother's heart. From birth, her mother, Eve, would endlessly share stories with her of the beauty of the Garden of Eden, and, while gently rocking her in her arms, would sing pleasant melodies filled with the stories of Eden. Mother and daughter, Evangeline, were never separated. What a wonderful mother-daughter relationship this was. Then one day it happened!"

While Ahira Naphtali was sharing this story with the people, Nathanael and Patience were sitting under their special redwood tree. Nathanael, along with all the people, were devoting their entire attention to every word that Ahira spoke. Patience, however, even though she heard every word, was not looking at Ahira. She had very firmly wrapped both her arms so tightly around Nathanael's chest that he could hardly breathe. Her head was over Nathanael's heart and she was quietly sobbing as she could hear Ahira tell of the motherly love and affection her mother Eve had for her.

As Ahira continues his story, he mentions that one day, as Eve and little Evangeline were playing in an open meadow, a large shadow seemed to engulf the beautiful sunshine above their heads. From, seemingly, out of nowhere a massive eagle with a wingspan of more than twenty feet, and giant talons, grasped little Evangeline and soared skyward. As this giant bird carried little Evangeline away, the words "Mama! Mama! Mama!" could be heard from the crying child. Mother Eve dropped to her knees, and with arms and eyes raised towards the sky, her heart broke as her eyes produced gushing rivers of sobbing tears. As Eve sobs her heart out, and gazes into the sky, it is as if the sky opened for the bird and her little girl and then closed up again. She never sees her firstborn child ever again! All she can hear is those final agonizing words from her sweet Evangeline, "Mama! Mama! Mama!"

As all, including Nathanael, are totally mesmerized by Ahira's words, Patience, with her head on Nathanael's chest, and firmly wrapped around him, is sniffling and crying softly "Mama! Mama!" Nathanael places his head on top of her head, and as he gently moves his hand through her thick auburn hair, he kisses the top of her head and whispers, "I love you my darling. It will be alright." As if not hearing his comforting words she continues to weep and cries, "Mama! Mama!"

In continuing his story, Ahira says that in that world, Eve was never the same again. She would go on to bare Adam many children who would become people of renown, but she seemed to be hollow, to see everything at a distance, as if to see with misty, glazed over eyes. She was never close to anyone ever again. For when that mighty bird carried away little Evangeline, the bird also carried away the loving, kind, gentle heart of her mother, Eve. Inside the little heart of Evangeline was her mother's very heart of love, goodness, and kindness, which Evangeline will treasure and carry with her all the days of her life. All Eve had for the rest of her days were those agonizing words, "Mama! Mama! Mama!" ringing in her ears as she could see that mighty bird carrying her little girl far away from her forever!

At this, Nathanael could feel Patience crying heavily on his chest and sobbing, "Mama! Mama!" in a way that all could hear. Everyone now looked at Patience with tear-filled eyes welling up in their faces. Truly this was an emotional time for everyone.

Ahira continued the story by saying that, "The place where this giant bird took little Evangeline was magical. It was a newly created world but apparently not filled yet. As the giant bird lands on a not-filled-yet land, the bird places Evangeline on the back of a reindeer who immediately runs to a predetermined location with little Evangeline clinging to the reindeer's back. Upon reaching a very humble abode, which in appearance resembled a large cave, two shining angels appeared. As they took little Evangeline off the reindeer, one of them carried her into the cave and placed her down at the feet of the presence of God. For the next two thousand years, in other world time, she sat at the feet of God, and without interruption, was taught by God Himself all the eternal truths and wisdom that God chose to teach her."

"Then one day, a special event happened. As a beautiful butterfly emerges from a chrysalis after a period of growth in the shelter of the chrysalis, this little girl was no longer a little girl! After two thousand years, she silently walked out of the front of the cave and appeared in all her God-provided beauty, as you see her today. Without saying a word she gently blew into the air causing a strong wind to blow in this created world not yet filled. She understood that God had now given her the name of Christian Nature and given her His authority and power to fill His creation with beauty made from the material He has provided her with. With the touch of God's finger in her finger, they will bring God's love, goodness, and kindness to all that God makes through us.' Thus, God gave Christian Nature the middle name of 'Patience.' It was God Himself who taught her wisdom, knowledge, and understanding. But it was her mother Eve's heart (which she will always cherish and carry with her), that taught her how to show wisdom, knowledge, and understanding through a heart of love, goodness, and kindness. Hence, God, in honor of her mother Eve, gave her the middle name of 'Patience,' which Christian Nature cherishes so dearly today."

With this, Nathanael places gentle kisses all over the top of Patience's head and slowly moves his hand through her hair and whispers, "O Patience, you are so sweet. How I love you so!" All he can hear, though, is her soft sniffling and "Mama! Mama!" The crowd takes in all of this enormous emotional moment and urgently desires to go to their queen and comfort her. But Ahira raises an index finger to them encouraging them to remain still and let Nathanael show his love for Patience and alone be her comfort at this time.

Ahira then continues his story by saying, "At that moment, Christian Nature begins to be obedient to God's instruction, to fill this created world with all the material that God has given her to fill it with." So with the knowledge, wisdom, and understanding of God saturating a heart seasoned with the love, goodness, and kindness of her mother, Patience went forth making a wonderful enchanted world. For you see, my dear friend, this is to be a world unlike any other world; a world that only exists in one's heart! A world specially created by God and filled by Christian Nature. This world is for all who give their hearts to God and come to live in this most beautiful of all worlds, that can only be seen with the eyes of one's heart."

This magical touch from the fingers of Christian Nature is amazing! In her heart's eye, she sees beauty and brings it out of her heart and into a world, which God gave her the power and authority to fill. Two thousand years before, this was an empty space, not existing in anyone's heart. Now she made it into the most beautiful of all lands. With the memories from her mother of what Eden looked like freshly in her heart, she sought to make this world just like the Eden in her heart. She began with the forest. Each and every tree specially touched by the kiss on the fingers from her heart. Grown from seeds, these wonderful trees grew in such a way that they provided comfort and encouragement to all whose lives they touched. She made flowers to put a smile on the face and joy in the heart of all who will see the flowers. Yes, my dear friends, God had given her the authority to make a beautiful new world of pure enchantment. From the grass in the meadows, to all animal life, to the mist and the dew on the ground, to the stars in the sky, to the dawning of each new morning, to the sunset every evening. Everything you can possibly imagine that provides comfort, joy, and happiness to all who see it from their heart, Christian Nature made in this beautiful garden of the heart!

As she carefully inspects one of her trees in this garden, her attention is focused on the only bird that she didn't make. She overwhelms the bird with an intense stare. This little two-inch bird must have felt great fear as this massive giant, this maker of all things in this magical land, Christian Nature, stares at it with a very intense face. Christian Nature says, "Come to me!" As Christian Nature holds out a finger this little bird comes and perches on it. She draws her finger to her face with the bird on it. With her eyes as big as the little bird itself she says, "By the authority of God I have made all animals in this land and yet I know that I did not make you! However, God has revealed to me who you are! You are that bird who took me from my mother and brought me here, aren't you?" With its head bowed low, it gave one tweet as if to say, "Yes." Christian Nature, with her deep blue-ocean-water eyes, looks into the bird's tiny eyes and says, "Thank you so very much! For what seemed to be so unbearably painful and impossible to deal with in the moment, in the long term, can bring forth the beauty of a flower designed to comfort and encourage all whom its life may touch. Through your obedience to God and doing what you did, all of this is now made available for all who will see from their heart the love, goodness, and kindness that God provides to all who truly give their heart to Him." In so doing, Christian Nature demonstrated the wisdom that God had taught her. Then she tells the bird that from this time forth, its name will be "Aeromore," who will always be with her until "Time" comes, at which point, Aeromore will be given by Christian Nature to Time as a token of her love for Time.

Ahira says, "Now it is time to talk about Time. While God was teaching Christian Nature, He had told her that there will be a time when God will provide her with the one who will magically possess the very heart of Christian Nature and will make you his own, and you will make him your own. At the time, she was taught that this one, who would possess her very heart, was four thousand years away from even being born in the other world. She was told that she must be patient though, because God's special gift to her had not yet arrived. Christian Nature, as a fully mature woman, could already feel her own heart beginning to yearn for this one who was still many years away from even being born. So, throughout the years, as Patience continued to individually make every item in this enchanted land (which can only be seen and inhabited in our heart), her own heart was beating briskly for the one who would possess her heart and have the most important role in the history of all creation, when combined with Christian Nature herself. She had asked God, 'How will I know when he arrives?' Patience came to understand that she will know when he comes and sits under her happy spot, under her special redwood tree. So it happened that each and every day, Patience would come and sit at her happy spot and give thanks to God for all He had done, look out over all this beautiful enchanted land, and yearn patiently for her heart's love. She would ponder: What would he look like? How will she know for sure it is he? Will he really love her? and many other things. She was told that when her 'Time' does come to her, she was to go to him and make known the ways of Christian Nature to him."

Ahira continued the story, "After many years, the day came, when an old man with thick, sparkling, silver-white hair came through this forest of life and quietly sat down underneath Christian Nature's special redwood tree, her 'happy spot.' She happened to be coming that particular moment to her happy spot for her special time. Little did she know that her special 'Time' had finally come, after all those years, come for her! She took a big gasp, put her hands over her mouth, her eyes become as large as dinner plates, and tears of joy started to flow as she realized that her very own Time had come to her as a gift from God! She could see him very clearly, but he could not see her because he had never seen from his heart before. She slowly walked up to him and walked around and around him studying every feature of this timeworn man. 'He is so handsome,' she said to herself. 'His eyes speak softness; his heart is so tender. His demeanor shows a genuine humility, gentleness, and a mysterious love for someone whom he still cannot see, but could feel in his heart.' It was as if she could feel his heart talking to her heart underneath the redwood tree, in her happy spot in the forest. She could feel his heart longing for hers and in the quietness of this natural moment, she reached forth with her lips and gave him an enchanted, soft, gentle kiss from the lips of one with tender hands, ever so gently caressing every inch of Nathanael Nobody's timeworn face. She then listened, as this one who will become 'Time' and will forever be one with Christian Nature, responded to the kiss by saying that, 'This was truly a magical kiss indeed, coming from the lips of one whom I cannot see, touched by hands which I can only feel, and mysteriously disguised by the breath of fresh air against my face.' To this, Christian Nature smiled and thought, 'Fresh air indeed!' She knew that her Time had come. Thus began the eternal love story of Time and Christian Nature. Two yet one!"

Chapter Six

The Journey

As the cleansing, renewing dawn of a fresh day enlightens the soul of a weary traveler, so the refreshing, healing, beginning of a new day gently wiped away the tears from the face of Patience. The miracle of this new day brings with it the excitement of the mystery that this day will have for them as Nathanael and Patience prepare to begin their journey to the dwelling place of God. Nathanael and Patience felt the need to thank the people by expressing to them that they are very grateful for the love and kindness that had been shown to them. They felt that if they did not show their gratitude to the people, it would be like wrapping a present for someone and then not giving it to them. So it is to feel gratitude toward someone and not show it. After this expression of gratitude, it was time to start their next adventure.

As Nathanael and Patience walk hand-in-hand and begin this journey together, Nathanael is amazed to see that the eyes in his head are not used nearly as much as the eyes in his heart. The eyesight from his heart now seemed more real to him than the external eyesight he had all his previous life in the, supposed, real world. Nathanael silently smiled to himself as he held Patience close and realized that back in the other world, which so many call the "real world," in truth, it is nothing more than a temporal dream in the eternal time of true reality. If all people would only trust Jesus Christ as their personal Savior from their sin, they would be invited to live in this created world of reality and develop the practice of seeing, hearing, and feeling with their heart. They could then live in this absolutely wonderful place of enchantment and beauty that can only be imagined.

Nathanael broke this spell of magical and musical silence by asking Patience if she really knew how they were going to get to where God dwells. She answered by saying, "I do not really know the way in my head at all, but my heart is very familiar with the way. We must always remember," she says, "that the true journey we take in life is not on some worn path that others feel they must travel. But the real journey is inside of you and we all must follow our own path rather than someone else's. God has made us one together. Remember, before you could see under our special redwood tree you felt our hearts beating as one. Our path together is as one, as it will be forever and ever. We are no longer two." As Nathanael and Patience continue their journey to the dwelling of God, they thoroughly enjoy the treasure that the wealth of each moment freely gives them. They arrive on a green clover, grass-filled mountain peak. They spread their arms far apart and whirl around and around, dancing and singing. Then they come together in an embracing hug and kiss. Nathanael says, "O my love, this is all so beautiful! I feel it all belongs to us. I feel that you and I are the queen and king of all that we see and that no one would deny us that privilege." Patience says, "That is so true, for you see we really don't have to own something to enjoy it. God has given this wonderful privilege to all. Everyone can enjoy God's wonderful creation without feeling that they personally have to own it."

Nathanael then begins to share with Patience the observations that the experiences of his life have taught him. "It seems that all persons choose to live in a world created by the imaginations, or dreams, that they see in their own hearts. We all create in our own heart what we choose to see, hear, and feel. Some choose to live in a world where the eyes of their heart only shows them vanity, greed, selfishness, hate, evil, violence, and every evil intent that can come out of a heart consumed with pride. This would be a horrible world to live in, a world in which everyone is always angry with everyone else, and consumed with bitterness, envy, and hatred. This world of their imagination towards all they see becomes their real world in which they choose to live."

"Some may say that this is all just my imagination; it is only taking place in my dreams, and is not really real. In the other world, there have always been 'dreamer' people called 'entrepreneurs' who have a heart, which controls the imagination of their mind and brings forth from that heart the birth of an idea to invent a particular object. Some would say that the invention was only in their heart and never was really 'real'. Their answer would be, 'Why not bring what is real in the heart out of the heart and make it real to others?' Because they have done this, the world has become a much better place. Each person's heart-controlled mind is like a blank canvas and we are each an artist, making real to others, what is real to us in our hearts! It is our own individual choice to put ourselves in the world we imagine. If we are honest with ourselves, our imagination in our own heart really is the world in which we choose to live. Some people may say that these worlds never really were. If they really look into their own heart though, they will see that their own heart has carried them off to another world also!"

Nathanael continues by adding that when he lived in the "other" world, he found that, "So many people called that strange world 'reality.' This is a world that everyone must walk in, where we must see, hear, and feel with our external eyes, ears, and hands. Even though we must walk, see, and hear with our eyes, ears, and hands, awake in that world, that is not the world in which we choose to live. In eternal reality, that world was really vacant. For everyone lives in their own world that was created in their heart that controlled their mind. Yes, we all walked with our external eyes open in the life we had in the other world, but I really do believe that everyone lives in their own personal worlds created in their hearts. Is not our life really what our heart-controlled thoughts make it?"

Nathanael continues to share his thoughts, "Everyone either chooses to live in their own personal dark world of evil in their hearts, or they can choose to live in this wonderful dream that has come true. A world created by God in the heart of each one who gives their heart to Jesus Christ as their personal Savior from sin. A world in which the Holy Spirit of God, shown as an allegory in the person of Patience, goes about filling a new heart with God's love, goodness, kindness, grace, and beauty for all who live in this world. Yes, this is a world more real than anything that has ever been created. It is the world in which I choose to live. I so wish that more and more people would live in this wonderful world that we call 'real' and would vacate the world of their anxieties and fears and come and live with us."

Patience then tells Nathanael that, "Soon after God started making all things beautiful in this world (through her), people began arriving. These people are those who gave their heart to God by faith and no longer use the eyes of their head as their primary means of sight. Now they look, hear, and feel, primarily, with their new heart. They still walk with eyes wide open in the other world, but their new world of reality was now in their new heart. As long as they were physically alive they lived here in their hearts, and then upon physical death, after Jesus died for their sins and rose again, they were taken to heaven. Thus, with just a few exceptions, Nathanael, all the people you have seen from your heart, here, are actually still alive in the other world, but their place of reality is here, living in their new heart."

For the longest time Nathanael and Patience just sat together holding hands in silence and gazing out and enjoying the beautiful views of all of God's creation. They drank deeply from the cup of wonder at living life as God intended. As they looked at all things with the eyes of their heart rather than with the eyes of their head, tears began to form in their eyes as they realized that there are so many people who choose to live in their own world of evil, greed, pride, envy, evil-speaking, and all sorts of vice, for these are the things that are regretfully real to them.

As Nathanael and Patience continue their journey, they listen and hear from their hearts' ears a wonderful sound of music, as if an artistically skilled orchestra was performing just for them. A close examination of the source proved to be a sweet sounding stream. As they listen to this natural talent they feel compelled to drink from this magical goblet of joy. As they do, they find each of their senses renewed with the freshness and purity of this God-provided treasure. After partaking of this stream they just listened in quietness to the enchanted sounds of natural music. Yes, my dear reader, the musical stream was sounding forth a melodious melody, the beautiful tall evergreen trees adding a magical intonation of their own, as the conductor herself, the gentle wind passed through the branches.

Patience shares with Nathanael the thought that it is wonderful what the heart can see when that heart is given to God and God enables one to see a beauty that some may never see. Nathanael smiles and says that he believes that Christian Nature has touched him! Then as they once again cuddle up next to each other, as Nathanael sees that twinkle in Patience's eyes and she says to him, "You have been touched by Christian Nature, my love, you have!" Nathanael gives Patience a kiss and says, "What a wonderful thing it is when one's sweetheart is Christian Nature herself!"

Nathanael tells Patience that it appears to him that all that he sees and hears, in this wonderful place of Christian Nature, seems to flow together slowly and yet in a very methodical manner. It is as if there is an unspoken secret it has that controls its very movement. As Nathanael pondered his thoughts in the golden silence of Time and listened to the soft breeze in the trees, the sweet voice of his love whispered in his ears, "Christian Nature's secret is patience, my love. Christian Nature's secret is patience!"

As Nathanael looks into the ocean-blue-eyes of Christian Nature, he cannot help but embrace her and thank God for giving to him the most wonderful gifts of all, with those gifts being eternal life in God Himself, and Christian Nature as a sweetheart endeared to him with the name "Patience."

As they slowly walk together, arm in arm, and enjoy the enchanted silence, they come to a not yet bloomed flower bud. Nathanael says to Patience, "This is strange. All of the other flowers are already blooming, but this one remains in the bud." With a twinkle in her eye, Patience says, "Maybe this one is waiting for Time to come to it." With that she tenderly touched the bud and immediately it bloomed into a Christian-Nature-touched rose, which produced a sweet fragrance for all to enjoy. She says, "Remember, there is never to be found any hurry in the world of Christian Nature, and yet when Time is added everything is accomplished!"

Nathanael comes to understand, in his heart, that the most important occurrences take place in the heart when we fall in love with Patience, and we become silent and listen to the voice of Patience, teaching us what is most important. Strange as it seems, Patience had taught him most when he had been silent!

Part Two

Nobody Learns His Lessons

Chapter One

Nobody Contemplates Who He Is

As the enchanted taste buds within the magical heart of Nathanael Nobody lovingly nibble at his tender mind, he begins to contemplate the significance of his own life. As he slowly, and with great care, reads with extreme interest each page of his life, he realizes that each page that he writes is like a chapter in the book of his life. He begins to understand that we each create our own worlds that we choose to live in. Each page of the artwork of our life is filled with precise details of the events of our life that took place on that particular page. At the fresh moment that those details were being painted on that particular page, they sometimes seemed very bad and uncomfortable. By the time the artwork of that page was complete though, a beautiful piece of work had been completed for God's glory and the benefit of all. It seemed that throughout his life none of the details of his life had been in vain. Each page in the artwork of his life seems to have had a purpose; and when the magic of Time and Patience had been added to it, what a truly enchanted life it had become! Now, as he walks through the forest of beautiful redwood trees, with each one having their own personal and unique beauty on display for all to see, he realizes that as each page of his own life was made up of a story in itself, those pages are now complete. He turns, now, to a new blank page and feels the excitement flowing through every cell of his being, eagerly waiting to be filled with the details of his new unfolding life. As Nathanael Nobody carefully ponders this, he silently smiles and wonders what this new life will consist of, in being "Time" himself. I suppose that only God and Time, himself, will tell!

Patience then speaks to Nathanael and tells him that God has chosen him, not because he is better than anyone else, but totally by God's grace. She tells him that God is about to give us His own personal authority to have the power to do what only Time and Patience can do. God has chosen us to help make everyone's world a beautiful path of flowers, rather than an ugly path of thorns, which so many people make for themselves.

Nathanael falls back on the soft redwood needle-covered ground of Christian Nature's own choosing, puts his hands behind his head, and looks up into the beautiful blue sky. "Oh Patience," he says, "You have carefully loved me and taught me how to truly find delight in all things. But remember, I am Nobody, Nathanael Nobody. I am nothing, certainly not an important person. You, Patience, you are Christian Nature. I am Nobody, nothing of significance! How is it really possible for someone like you to love someone like me?"

Patience simply smiled, took his hands, looked into his eyes, which now had tears in them, and said, "That is why God has chosen you to be Time, my forever-love. For in your own heart you will always see yourself as being Nobody. We would all be so much wiser if each day we would but look into the touchstone of truth, and see ourselves as we really are! It is because of this that God will use you in a way that you have never been used before. From this moment on, you will not only see with your own heart, but also with mine. I will not only see with my heart, but also with yours. We are forever each others: I am forever yours and you are forever mine!"

As they once again resume their journey to God, Christian Nature shares many things with Time. Nathanael comes to understand that Time will become the primary teacher of all mankind in every world. All people will look to Time to understand the meaning of life itself. God will provide Time with wisdom to teach others how to make right choices in life. Time must always remember, though, that he is Nobody, and that all of this comes not from him but from God. Nathanael cannot help but say, "It seems I have lost the world I spent so long living in and been recreated to live in a new world I never thought possible." As Nathanael and Patience draw closer to the dwelling of God, Nathanael notices a soft, gentle, tap, tap, tap on his heart. He mentions to Patience this strange sensation and tells her he may be on the verge of what they call a "heart attack" in the other world. Patience smiles, snuggles up next to him and says, "That is not a heart attack. That gentle knock on your heart's door is God seeking admittance into your heart. Even though you have already trusted Him as your personal Savior, this is a special visit."

Strange as it may seem, Nathanael comes to realize that it is not they who are coming to visit God, but rather God who is visiting them! As Nathanael and Patience continue to share their thoughts, he comes to learn that it is only from God, and God alone, that any form of true wisdom can ever be found. In the other world, it seems that no one really comes to understand this truth. If anyone gains any understanding of this truth in their heart, it is because God, Himself, has taught this to their heart.

Nathanael finds his heart filled with anxiety as he falls to the ground and begins to sob great tears of sorrow. He cries to Patience, "I am a very foolish man. I have never had any form of wisdom in my life at all. My name is rightly called 'Nobody,' for I am truly nothing of significance at all. My own heart, mind, and eyes all bear witness to each other that I am not a wise man and yet you share these things with me about the privilege of being 'Time' himself. There has never, ever been a human less deserving of this privilege than myself. The fact that God would even spend His time with me is totally incomprehensible to me!"

Patience simply smiled with that special twinkle in her eye and said, "My love, did you hear what you just said? For you see, it is because of what you just said, coming right out of your new heart, that God has chosen you to be His special 'Time.' It is His grace that has brought you to this special moment in your life. Do you not think He has heard every word you have said and smiles over your honesty about yourself?"

With that they arrive at God's very simple and humble dwelling. Nathanael is shocked at the humbleness and simplicity found at the dwelling place of the Creator of all things. Patience, seeing Nathanael shocked says, "What did you expect? God can dwell in whatever dwelling

He chooses, but my heart tells me that the Holiest of all, the Creator of all, the Redeemer of our souls, will possibly use this humble surrounding as a tool to teach us some valuable lessons that we need to learn and understand in our heart."

Chapter Two

Nobody Begins to Learn

As the eyesight of Nathanael Nobody's heart intensely studies the humble dwelling place of God, it appears to him that God chooses to dwell in the natural world of His own creation. Nathanael notices that carefully concealed, yet open to all, in the middle of the trunk of an enormous redwood tree was an open door. "Does God really live in a tree?" Nathanael thought. But no, this was no ordinary tree. A truly magical and enchanted tree it was indeed! Its external appearance, more than one thousand feet in circumference, was quite literally touched by the patient hand of Christian Nature herself. Each feature, in its own unique beauty, specifically pointing to God as if to say, "There is no beauty in me; if there is any, it is God's." What incredible beauty there is to see! The sweet sounds of the multi-colored birds singing their melodies of happiness; each one singing their own life story while the little babies in their nests seek to mimic the sweet sounds of their parents. There are many lives of many creatures that make their skillfully crafted homes underneath the protective bark of God's natural protection for them. Nathanael cannot help but notice that each branch of the tree itself was used by its Creator for the purpose of providing support for an innumerable congregation of God-dependent creatures. The life in each branch carefully providing a home and nourishment to its inhabitants, in much the same way as a God-provided church provides a home and place of nourishment for other God-created creatures.

Yes, my dear reader, God, in His wisdom always knows where to dwell and it seems that He chooses to dwell in abodes that are not necessarily some beautiful, luxurious, spacious, mansions that may be pleasing to the vain external eyes of man. Rather, He chooses to dwell in the simple, humble, non-attention-getting locations that only exist in the hearts of those who seek him.

As Nathanael and Patience slowly enter through the bloodstained door of God's heart, they realize that the only eternal, true teacher of all only appears when each student is ready to listen! Patience tells Nathanael not to look into the face of God but rather to bow at His feet and stay in that position until told to do otherwise. As they enter and bow at the very nail-scarred feet of God, great tears begin to flow from the loving eyes of both Patience and Nathanael. The teardrops from the deep ocean-blue-eyes of Patience fall on the feet of God as she lovingly wipes them with her thick beautiful auburn hair. Nathanael cries out, "Oh great Teacher, I know nothing! Please teach us what we need to know to accomplish your purpose in our lives!"

God then begins His awakening of the heart of Nathanael to discover that the lessons that his life has taught him had to be personally lived before he could understand their meaning. If he will but listen to the voice of all that happens to him in his life, he will find that nothing that has ever happened has been a waste of time. Every occurrence that has left a footprint on his life is like an ingredient that has served a purpose in the product produced in his life. He must make every ingredient count, for each occurrence, like an ingredient, adds its own flavor to the nutritional morsel that his life produces for the glory of God and the enjoyment of others. God shares with him that it appears that all of humanity wants to be happy. But the real secret, the key that unlocks the door of their heart to the world of happiness only happens when they take a real interest in all the details of their simple, ordinary, personal lives.

Nathanael comes to understand that as Time, it will be his purpose to come alongside of people and teach them these truths. Nathanael says, "How much better it is to get your wisdom, O Holy One, than to get all the gold in the world; and to understand these things is more valuable than all silver" (Proverbs 16:16). "O God," Nathanael says, "My heart is overflowing with joy over your knowledge and wisdom that you are awakening this unworthy creature to."

Nathanael says to God that the more his desire to please God with his life increases, it seems the less likely he is to set his foot into a trap that would jeopardize his well-being. It appears that the more intense his love grows for God, the deeper his thirst grows for drinking from the fountain of life. As Nathanael's thirst and appetite grow for the knowledge that God awakens him to, it seems as if his mouth is being filled with the delicious, nutritional, sweet taste of a honey-filled honeycomb. It is as if God is hand-feeding Nathanael the knowledge of His wisdom. As Nathanael feeds on God's wisdom, he thinks God must really love him to spend His time to nurture Nathanael's heart and soul. Nathanael is consumed with the eternal truth that he is not worthy of the least of all of the truths that God has revealed to him (Genesis 32:10). "What a wonderful place for a human heart to dwell," Nathanael thought. "Dwelling at the very nail-scarred feet of God; drinking from God's fountain of knowledge; and being hand-fed with the sweet taste of God's wisdom! I could stay here forever," he thought as he sobbed great tears of joy.

Chapter Three

The Lesson from Mistakes

As Nathanael Nobody thoroughly enjoys the sweetness of this time in the presence of God, he is consumed with the desire to no longer waste even the slightest moment of life on selfish pursuits. From this moment on, his desire is to devote his life to demonstrating to God how grateful he is for all God has done for him. In the midst of this happiness, a certain sorrow envelopes him, a sadness over how much of his life he has already wasted in selfish pursuits. Nathanael comes to understand that he has no control over what has already happened to him in his past. All he has to do now is decide what to do with the time that is still given to him. He realizes that he can't change his past, but he can learn from it, and he can change the way he views it.

Nathanael seems to be riding an emotional roller coaster, from enjoying mountaintop experiences of happiness of being taught by God Himself, to descending into the depths of depression as he, then, dwells upon the blunders he has been defined by. God awakens him to understand the value that his mistakes of his past can give to him. He comes to understand that there is tremendous eternal worth and value to be positively experienced in the net worth of his life, if he will but learn the lesson, today, that those mistakes are trying to teach him. It seems like those individual mistakes that Nathanael has made all his life are like teachers in a classroom, who are doing their best to teach this wayward student a lesson that will greatly benefit his future, if he will learn it. Nathanael cannot help but gently smile and think, "I must certainly have had a lot of instructors in my life!" Nathanael's heart reveals to him that this is, indeed, wise and valuable instruction! To be taught by our own past mistakes is true wisdom, if we will learn from these instructors! He says to God that the instructive mistakes he has made in his past have left some very painful wounds in his heart that seem to never really heal. God shows him how he can let those wounds be his instructors. For those wounds have the earnest desire to teach you wisdom. Nathanael says, "How is that, O Holy One?" God enlightens his understanding by showing him that all the mistakes of his past, all the wounds that he has inflicted on himself, all of the instruction of his past has come together to teach him that, if he will learn from all of this instruction, he will be more likely to see farther into the future. If we will all look with our heart intently into our past and learn from it, we will greatly enhance the value of what is to come.

As Nathanael dwells on these thoughts and reasons with his heart on the significance of this valuable teaching from God, he silently smiles and says, "If I will learn from all these instructors I have had in my life and from God Himself, maybe, just maybe, Time might be used to bring glory to God, and wisdom to all who will learn from the mistakes we have all made in our past."

As Nathanael ponders these things, he realizes that he can't let the valuable instructors of his past mistakes take away from the value of his present moment. They are there to help him, not hurt him! He realizes that he has already been forgiven of his past sins. So he shouldn't loiter on past mistakes; he needs to learn from them and then live in the beauty of the new moment for the glory of God and the benefit of others."

Nathanael comes to realize the wisdom in seeking to not repeat those mistakes. He saw the importance of not being shackled by past mistakes, but starting each day fresh with the experience of the past permanently inscribed on his heart. This is sort of like staying out of a dangerous rushing river that would result in one's destruction. The past experience of a mistake has already taught him, that, except for God's Grace, that past mistake of going into that dangerous river could have cost him his life!

God then shares with Nathanael the value of experience, saying that, but for the wise instruction of mistakes that have personally taken the time to teach him important lessons, he would never have the rich wealth of experience to freely give away to others. We must remember that all the time that we have made bad choices in our past, if we have learned from these instructors, we will have had the wealth of 'experience' put to our account. Now if we will invest this into making good judgments in the future, we can truly provide the valuable riches of wisdom, which has its ultimate source in God alone, to bring glory to God and benefit to all who will learn from their mistakes of the past.

Nathanael sees that as Time, one of his primary purposes will be to take people back into their past that they may learn from it, enhance the worth of their present, and let them get a glimpse of what their future may be like if they live for the glory of God and the benefit of others.

"What a wonderful lesson this has been!" thought Nathanael. "What a privilege to sit at the feet of God Himself, being hand-fed with the sweetness of His teaching; to understand that God has carefully designed everything in my life to be for His Glory." Nathanael cries to God and says "Thank You! O God, please use this insignificant life to be a benefit to others!"

Chapter Four

The Lesson of Being Thankful and Grateful

The eyes of Nathanael Nobody's heart are beginning to understand just how very important it is to be thankful for all God has given to him, and to show this thankfulness in the form of deeds of gratitude. So many times in his life he has thought to say "thank you" to others for actions that have benefited him, but had not actually done so. In much the same way, he has thought to say "thank you" to God, but seldom did.

He begins to understand that just as people appreciate acts of thankfulness by others toward them when they make a sacrifice of themselves to help other people, God also appreciates our spoken thankfulness to Him for what He has done for us. Some may say that sacrificial acts that benefit others, should not receive the gift of thankfulness because it came from a heart that only wanted to be used to help others, and was not expecting a gift of thankfulness. However, to not say "thank you" would be like demonstrating to that person that what they did for your benefit has no value for you at all. How many times have so many people never told God "thank you" for the gift that personally cost Him so much on the Cross! This costly gift to us was freely given for our benefit, and yet we seldom say "thank you!" To take this gift for granted and not say "thank you" is a great sin indeed! To not say "thank you" to anyone who makes a sacrifice of themselves to benefit us, could this not also be called a sin?

God has given each person the same amount of hours, minutes and seconds each day. Can we not use at least some of them to find a reason to say "thank you" to someone who has helped us that day? We owe so many people the gifts of thankfulness and gratitude for sacrifices made on our behalf. Showing gratitude could be like repaying the first installment on a debt. If we choose to not pay on what we owe, the day may come when we would someday be foreclosed upon! If we choose to not show gratitude or appreciation, it could be like letting a valuable life insurance policy expire. If we do not renew that friendship every once in a while, we may run the risk of losing it.

God then begins to show to Nathanael the difference between thankfulness and gratitude, for they are not the same thing. Thankfulness is usually shown in the form of words, which is proper and good. Gratitude is shown in supporting those thankful words with acts. It is interesting that we all have physical hearts that really aren't very big. But it is amazing just how much gratitude towards others these little hearts can hold if we will fill our heart with this priceless treasure!

Nathanael comes to understand that God has incredibly blessed his insignificant life. All the remaining days of his life he desires, from this point on, to be grateful to God and to others in both words and deeds, and not to be an unthankful fool!

During all the time that Nathanael was being taught by God and reawakened to truths that he had forgotten, the love of his heart, Patience, had been silently sitting right next to him, holding his hand and quietly sobbing over the privilege she had of being where she was. She truly loves God and loves Nathanael dearly and tenderly, and has been obedient to all that God had led her to do. Nathanael has been so absorbed with his love for God in this instruction by God to him, that he had totally neglected this dear sweetheart, who has devoted her life to teaching him what God had taught her. It begins to dawn on Nathanael that maybe she is crying because, all of a sudden, he has neglected her. Nathanael then stops, looks into the beautiful blue-ocean-water crying eyes of Patience, embraces her with all his strength, and tells her thank you for allowing herself to be used by God to make such a difference in his insignificant life. If it weren't for her, he would not be where he is. With eye-to-eye and nose-to-nose, he holds the sweetheart of his life in his arms and tells her thank you for loving him as she does. Patience then totally loses control and sobs great tears of joy as she and Nathanael emotionally hug each other, tenderly, in the presence of God. Yes, my dear reader, may we all learn to take the time to say "thank you" and express, with deeds of gratitude, the love for those who have made a difference in our lives through the sacrificial acts of love they have shown toward us.

God shares with both Nathanael and Patience that even though they truly love each other, when they show love and gratitude toward each other, it is as if they are showing great respect towards each other also.

This incredible love story, which has carefully unfolded with Nathanael Nobody and Christian Nature, in the person of Patience, has blossomed like a beautiful flower with its sweet fragrance filling the air, in the form of true love! As they both are consumed with a heart filled with love, thankfulness, and gratitude toward God, they have shown it with their heart overflowing with love, thankfulness, and gratitude toward each other, as they seek to please God together, as if they are one. For you see, my dear reader, when Time and Christian Nature are totally consumed with a thankfulness toward God, which they are, there is no limit to how they can be used by God to bring great benefit to you!

Chapter Five

The Lesson from Forgiveness

"What a joyous experience of partaking of wholesome, nutritious, substantive food this has been," thought Nathanael Nobody. "Just to be the recipient of enjoying the privilege of being personally hand-fed by God, Himself, with the delectable food of His choosing, is truly like feasting at a banquet table prepared and set by God! Is it really possible for life to be better than this?"

After reviewing in his heart what God has already revealed to him about how to take the mistakes of his past, bring the birth of experience out of the labor of his mistakes, and then use that experienced new life to bring practical wisdom to others, Nathanael is awestruck by the wonderfulness of God. As he gives thanks to God for all God has done for him, he reflects on how forgiving God has been to him all the days of his life. As God reads Nathanael's heart, He sees that the time has now come for Nathanael to be awakened to understand the value of forgiveness. Nathanael comes to understand that as God has forgiven us of our sins, or mistakes, so we should adopt a lifestyle-habit of forgiving others.

We need to look at our heart and mind as sort of a balance sheet. Just as a person would carefully study their own personal financial balance sheet to adopt the practice of having a healthy financial budget, so one should carefully study their own personal relational balance sheet that they have in regards to forgiveness. We all must realize that no thought just sits in our heart free of charge. Each thought we have will be either paying us as an "asset" or costing us as a "liability." If a thought is filled with the sweetness of being willing to forgive others of wrongs done to us, then it will bring gain to us, much like God forgave us! If the thought is proud, and will not forgive others, it is like the bitterness of a poison plant that will bring sickness to our heart and mind, and could result in the death to our heart and mind. Forgiving thoughts flowing freely from the heart to the mind are like assets that bring profit to us. Unforgiving thoughts are like liabilities that bring harm to us. We must realize that these thoughts directly affect our feelings, which have a direct result shown in the way we act toward the one who we should be forgiving. Thus, a spiritually 'wealthy' person is actually one who is poor in spirit, humble in heart and has a constant desire to forgive others' wrongs that have been done towards them. Nathanael thinks to himself that God is truly wealthy in wisdom, for He has a strong "asset" column and no liability column at all! O that we would all have such an income statement of forgiveness towards others that would bring glory to God and the benefit of forgiveness towards others!

God shares with Nathanael, that, if he would, at all times, have a true willingness to forgive others, that God would give him the ultimate victory in all things that apply to life and happiness. Once again, it appears that God has freely given to Nathanael a special key that unlocks and opens the door that leads into a wonderful world of true happiness!

Nathanael comes to understand that God places an extremely high value on those who are willing to forgive others. Even though this highly valued gift is of great importance, its cost is actually nothing if we will only humble ourselves and not be filled with the sin of pride.

Not only is there great value in this gift of forgiveness that we freely give to others, but we also need to consider the worth of this key that can unlock the prison cell that we put ourselves into and has the ability to set us free. For if we do not forgive others, we will just sit in the prison cell that we have made for ourselves and have no way out. Yes, we will just sit there until we realize that God has given us the key to get out. It is in our pocket and we can get out any time we want if we will only forgive others. Yes, indeed, my dear reader, a great adventure can be had by all of us if we will are willing to forgive others the wrongs that they have done to us. If God, Himself, was, and is, constantly willing to forgive us, can we not be willing to always forgive others? A wonderful God-given adventure awaits us if we are willing to do this!

When God forgives He also forgets. Maybe we would be demonstrating some wisdom if we realized, that, to be wronged is really nothing of significance, unless we continue to remember it and let it imprison us in our cell of unforgiveness.

God enlightens Nathanael's heart to think about the beauty and the sweet fragrance of joyous flowers. It seems that everything about flowers is attractive to our senses. In spite of their beauty though, some people enjoy stomping all over them and doing whatever possible to destroy them. In spite of the fact that mean people are always doing them wrong and seeking to destroy them, they continue to be forgiving, even though they are wronged. After a thorough stomping of the sweet flowers under their feet, these people walk off with a proud heart. What they don't realize, though, is that the sweet scent of forgiveness is on their boots and the flower they sought to destroy has already forgiven them! For you see, the flower always forgives and leaves the sweet scent of forgiveness, even upon the vilest of persons!

So God concludes His lesson of forgiveness with Nathanael by encouraging him to be like His beautiful sweet flowers: no matter what kind of a stomping he takes in life, he should always respond with the sweet scent of forgiveness; and to not only forgive, but to see the benefit of also totally forgetting the transgression against him.

Chapter Six

The Lesson from Habits

There are countless people who have traversed the many paths through this adventure called "life." Each person, if asked, would have loved to enjoy the privilege of looking into a crystal ball and seeing what their future would look like. Little do people realize that in a strange way, each of us have been given an opportunity with our life to predict our own future. We can 'reinvent' or 'recreate' ourselves if we will take the blueprint that God gives to us, instructing us how we should live, and then give birth to that new life with the reproduction of it in our own heart.

As Nathanael Nobody reviews what he has already been enlightened to, he comes to understand the significance of what he has been taught: the lesson of letting the mistakes of his past be valuable instructors, teaching him and showing him the wisdom to be gained from his past experiences; the lesson about showing thankfulness and gratitude towards those who have made a difference in his life; also seeing with his heart the importance of, just as God has forgiven us of our transgressions, we should also forgive others when we have been wronged.

It is then that God performs an intricate delicate surgery upon the tender heart of Nathanael. He places a magical and enchanted device directly above his heart that will enable him to pace himself through the course of his life, and constantly apply these truths to his daily life. If he will do this, he will find that the future, which always comes as a gift one day at a time, will, in some ways, be able to be predicted. He comes to understand that as he starts each day fresh, each day will be like a blank sheet of paper. He will seek to break one bad habit and to give birth, as a mother to a child, to one good habit. He starts to understand that he will become what he repeatedly does. He realizes that he needs to pay special attention to these new children that he has called "habits," that we all frequently give birth to, and do all he can to make sure they are children he can be proud of.

Nathanael comes to understand just how strong an influence habits can have on us. Even though we may be the parent who actually gave birth to the habit, through the course of time, that habit often remakes us! We often find that the influence of a habit sometimes becomes stronger upon us than so-called "common sense reasoning."

God enlightens Nathanael's understanding to seeing, from his heart, the value of firmly establishing "good habits." For when we firmly establish a habit in our lives, it is hard to resist its strong pull upon us. Nathanael asks God, "How can I give birth to the child of good habits in my heart?" He understands that it comes by practicing, every day, what he already knows. Always remember the value of: mistakes, experience, wisdom; the worth of thankfulness to others; and the treasure to be found in forgiving others. Nathanael comes to see that as he practices these universal truths, one day at a time, and keeps it up each day of his life, he will eventually become proficient at it. He must remember, though, that with each day, a little weed of potential bad practice could grow into a "bad habit" in his own garden of life. It is important not to neglect that weed, but pull it up and get rid of it! If he does not get rid of it when it is small, that little weed could get large and soon become a strong bad habit wreaking havoc in his beautiful garden.

Nathanael comes to see the importance of being poor in spirit, of being truly humble, and yet possessing the strength of being remarkably strong in regards to uprooting the bad habits that try to establish a stronghold in his life. Just as a body builder spends much time building muscle to make himself strong for the assaults that each day may bring upon him, so we must each become strong body builders in our heart, to withstand the daily assaults that the potential bad practices might try to establish in our own lives.

He understands that one truly strong good habit, that is constantly used, has the power to overcome a weak bad habit, that is becoming weaker every day! He realizes that it is important to let these well-used strong habits mold us, for if they do, they will build good character traits within each of us.

Nathanael's heart begins to see that habits are sort of like chains, which at first seem very weak, so weak that we can hardly feel them. Eventually, though, they become so strong through use that they cannot be broken. We are quite literally bound by them! Yes, regretfully we weave a bundle of these strong chains each day and eventually we cannot break it!

Nathanael sees that as Time, himself, he will have the responsibility to come alongside of others and enlighten each one to the treasure of learning from their past mistakes. Then, teaching them to take the experiences they have gained, and through God-given wisdom, taught by Time, taking that wisdom and developing good habits in the present, which will help them to see farther into how their future may be born. "Truly," Nathanael says, "This has, indeed, been a lesson filled like a treasure chest with eternal, valuable riches!"

Chapter Seven

The Lesson from Anger

As the enlightenment from the Holiest of all penetrates deep into the recesses of Nathanael Nobody's heart, the eternal truth of what God awakens him to, breaks through and into the shaft of his heart in much the same way that one who is hiding a rich treasure would break into the shaft of a mine and hide a valuable treasure chest of wealth. Only, in this case, it is God who is bringing the treasure and depositing it in the deep recesses of Nathanael's heart.

As Nathanael opens up this treasure chest, he is once again enlightened to, yet, another nugget of eternal wisdom that God is giving to him. As he studies this valuable jewel, he sees himself coming to a fork in the road of his life. He has a choice to make: he can choose to practically apply wisdom in his life and be willing to forgive others, or he can choose to be proud and not forgive others. He can be wise or foolish – the choice is his alone to make!

God now shares with him what would happen if he chooses to be foolish, to fill his heart with a supposed "justified" anger and not forgive others. For you see, each person has the power within his or her own tongue to either kill a person, or to give life to a person. Each person, with the power of the tongue, can either drive their sharp, two-edged sword through the heart of another and kill both that person and themselves, or they can leave that sharp sword in its scabbard and use the soothing balm of comforting, forgiving words to bring health to the one in need of forgiveness (Proverbs 12,18). This is sort of like being a tree. When others pluck a fruit off of our tree and eat it, does it bring health and comfort to them, or is the fruit from our tree filled with anger, bitterness, and unforgiveness toward those whom we feel have wronged us?

There is a correlation in our lives between pride and anger, versus humility and forgiveness. Just as in extreme floods there are some trees that, as if they are showing humility, voluntarily bend, and because they bend they not only survive, but also in many cases, go on to prosper. There are other trees, though, that when the extreme flooding comes, they, in pride, refuse to bend to wrongs done to them, as if in anger. Because of this, these stubborn trees are torn up roots and all. Such is the person who is poisonously possessed with anger and pride!

We are all what our heart-controlled mind makes us! If our heart is filled with the poisonous toxin of pride and anger, it will poison our mind and our entire body and produce an unhealthy person. Some may reason in their poisonous toxin-consumed heart that they have a legitimate reason to be angry. Maybe we should ask ourselves, "Is it really worth destroying the purity of forgiveness, the good health of a clean heart, and helping others to be angry?" If we choose to be angry, we would be poisoning our own heart, destroying ourselves as we destroy others. We would bring great harm to others and ourselves through our proud and angry ways. Yes, when we will not cease from our anger, we not only hurt others, but ourselves as well. We need to truly think before we speak! O that our words would be forgiving, healthy, healing words, and not proud, angry, destructive words!

So many times when we lie down on our beds and try to sleep, we find that this is impossible because we are consumed with an anger that we cannot forget. It is as if we are lying in bed and carefully making plans for a journey of revenge, making plans to get even for wrongs done to us. If we choose to go ahead and do this, maybe we should just dig two graves: one for the person we are seeking to kill with our angry words, and the other for ourselves, who we will have sacrificed in the process!

So, is the reason we are angry really worth destroying that person and losing our effectiveness in seeking to help others? It is interesting to note that we will not actually be punished for our anger, for we all get angry from time to time. We need to let the soothing, wise balm of being willing to forgive, heal that hurt. The problem is that it is the anger itself, if not wisely dealt with, that will inflict great punishment on our unforgiving hearts!

So, as Nathanael Nobody stands at the fork in his road of life, the one he comes to every day, he must listen to his heart. If he chooses to be unforgiving and angry with others for wrongs done to him, he will go down the path that not only destroys the other person, but also himself. If he chooses to be forgiving and kind, he will go down the path that leads to happiness at being used by God to bring glory to God and benefit to others. Nathanael gives thanks to God for the privilege of opening up another treasure chest filled to overflowing with precious jewels of wisdom. He decides that there is a whole lot more worth and value in being forgiving of others than in the "fools gold" of being angry and proud. As God tells him, "Anger resides in the bosom of fools!" (Ecclesiastes 7:9).

Chapter Eight

The Lesson from Kindness

Nathanael and Patience awake at the very feet of Holy God to a new chapter in their book of life. They both feel a fresh excitement at the valuable treasure of what God has for them on this day. Such is the enlightenment that each person can feel if they will only start each morning fresh, sitting at the feet of God, listening intently to God's instructions to them. It is as if Nathanael and Patience start each day without any anxiety and greatly anticipate the adventure that God has for them on this most important of all days. For you see, as we arise each morning, if we will anticipate with fresh zeal what the dawning of the new day brings with it, we will find that each day has the potential to be the best day of our life! The key is to start it by listening, intently, at the feet of God!

With this eagerness and anticipation coursing through their veins, today, they both come to see the wisdom in being a farmer. Farmers rise extremely early each morning. They do not, necessarily, look or even expect each day to actually produce a bountiful harvest for them. They are very patient about what they do with their time and they hold themselves personally accountable for what they do with their time. They see the wisdom in carefully and precisely planting valuable seeds, which in time and with much patience fulfill their purpose of bringing glory to God and benefit to others. Let us see the value in each day, planting the patient seeds of kindness, that they may provide eventual benefit to all who will partake of the fruit from them. This nutritional fruit of kindness is a treasure that grows from the seeds that we plant. God shares His wisdom with Nathanael and Patience by telling them the value of realizing the importance of the impact that their lives can have on others. It is imperative that we plant, as farmers, the patient seeds of kindness in our own lives. Eventually those seeds grow into mature trees filled with the fruits of kindness that all people want to eat.

As many animals gather under fruit-bearing trees to partake of their kindness each morning, may others look forward to gathering around us each day, to partake of our kindness which, hopefully, will have a profound impact on their own lives for the day.

Nathanael and Patience come to understand that a very treasured fruit that others would love to eat off of our kindness-tree each morning would be a simple smile! Everyone loves to taste another person's genuine smile! Nothing tastes better than a true smile. It says "pleasure" to the taste buds of all as they thoroughly enjoy each moment of this treat that you are providing for them. So, always, freely, give each person you meet the delicious fruit of a genuine smile, for it is truly the universal language of kindness!

With each moment of each day, let the mature fruit of your kindness-tree also contain precious acts of kindness for all to partake of. Every day presents each one of us many opportunities to do just simple acts of kindness towards others, which costs us nothing, and yet, may be just what another person may really need that day. You see, each person, every day, is experiencing the ravaging effects of doing battles, and if we freely give to them the cherished fruit of a smile, and a kind deed for their benefit, it may help them dearly in the personal battles they are dealing with that day. Kind words, like seeds, are never thrown away. They will always bear the fruit of kindness towards those they are freely given to.

We must come to understand that each one of us are not only farmers, patiently planting seeds of kindness to grow into mature trees providing the fruit of kindness for the benefit of others, but we are also architects. As an architect carefully, methodically and with precision develops the intricate details of every inch of a building, we are to do the same with our lives. Our own personal fate, the precise details of every inch of our life, is precisely determined by what our heart produces in our life. If our heart, the architect of our life, under the guidance of God, produces the habitual practice of kindness, then the building of our life can truly be a blessing towards all who will use it.

Nathanael's and Patience's hearts are enlightened to understand that wherever the path of their lives may lead them each day, they always need to have the eyes of their heart wide open to look for kindness opportunities.

God shares with Nathanael and Patience that some people feel that they are useless in this world and that they have nothing that they can offer to others. What they don't realize, though, is that if they allow themselves to be used by God to share the fruit of kindness to others, they may find themselves being used by God greatly to lighten the burden of someone else. Each person must realize that they are unique! No matter how old they are or what their circumstances may be, they still have that special gift of kindness that can be freely given away to greatly benefit another person. This gift of kindness can be given to others no matter how old one may be! Yes, indeed, just the simple little thought of sharing kindness with another person has more value in it than just giving away a large amount of money. It doesn't take a great deal of effort to share kind words and deeds, but their long-term effect can bear endless precious benefits to another person. Each one, if they really want to be a blessing of encouragement to others, needs to begin this fruitful venture of sharing kindness today! If one chooses not to share kindness today, tomorrow may be too late to help that person who needed your help today. This act of kindness that you desire to show may be just what they need to receive the healthy balm for their soul and the blessing they urgently need today.

No matter what the day may bring, no matter what the injuries and events of the day may bring upon another, it is always possible to show kindness. God awakens the understanding of Nathanael and Patience to see with their hearts' eyes that when others see that you are full of kindness, they will see it shining in your eyes like the sun at noonday. They will see it in the way that you look at all things with tender, delicate and loving eyes. They will see and hear it in the way you talk to others and in the way you conduct yourself. There will be absolutely no way that you will be able to hide it, for it will overflow in your life like a magical goblet filled, to overflowing, with enchanted drops of golden comfort.

"Oh what wonderful enlightenment the Holy One has shared with us this day!" thought Nathanael. These are mighty truths that we have always known, that we should make as everyday practices, yet we so seldom practice them. Oh to be wise and realize the difference between having the knowledge of what we should do, and the wisdom to actually apply what we know to be true, to bring glory to God and benefit to the lives of others! Yes, my dear reader, we should always, patiently, plant the seeds of kindness in the soil of our heart each day, that they might grow into mature trees providing the fruit of kindness which brings glory to God and health-providing benefits towards all whom our lives may touch.

Chapter Nine

The Lesson of Happiness

The gift of God's wisdom that He has awakened Nathanael and Patience to during this special visit, has totally saturated their hearts like a sponge absorbing all the water around it. It appears that, as a sponge fully absorbs a bucket full of water, the very heart of an all-wise God has fully absorbed their own hearts. It is as if God reads their hearts and understands that, for the moment, their hearts have absorbed all the wisdom that God has given to them.

What a treasure-chest of wealth that God has given to them! Very similar to the feeling that one would have upon receiving the full benefits of a highly nutritious meal, they were contentedly happy and filled to overflowing with joy. God understands their happiness as He carefully puts all these lessons together in a special container called their "hearts." As He directs their attention to the ribbons around the gift and finalizes it with a beautiful bow, He tells them that the ribbons and bow represent the true happiness that will come to them, if they treasure these lessons in their hearts all the days of their lives. For when the heart is under the control of wisdom-lessons from God, one will find that there is real meaning to life and that each person would have a real reason to live. The reason to live should always be to bring glory to God and benefit to others.

So, is it really possible to live happily ever after? Nathanael comes to understand that the answer is a very emphatic, "Yes!" if one's heart is consumed to overflowing with being used by God to be a true benefit to others.

While sitting at the feet of God, Nathanael and Patience now spend some time conferring among themselves. They talk about all that has taken place since they entered the dwelling of God's heart, in the humble abiding place of His choosing: the lesson of learning from the instructive mistakes of their past, and letting those mistakes give birth to the child of experience that will grow to make wise choices in life as a result of being a child born of experience; the value of being willing to forgive others' wrongs done to us in much the same way as God forgives us; the value of giving thanks to God and others who have made great sacrifices of themselves for our benefit; the value of kindness towards all that others might see God's kindness through us; and the fruit of encouragement to all whom our lives may touch. Many have said it, and it is so true, that we can all be happy, indeed, when what we consistently think, say, and do are all in harmony!

Before concluding this visit, God gives them a very serious warning. He tells them that in the other world, there are many who invest the time of their short life in doing the very opposite of taking heed to the sound advice of God. They never do pay attention to the instructors who are trying to teach them from the mistakes of their past. They continue to be strong-willed, proud, and, in practice, not desiring to learn from their mistakes. They do not feel a need to give thanks or express gratitude to anyone for the sacrifices made by others for their benefit. They feel that the giving of thanks to others is a weakness, and something that a proud heart should never, under any circumstances, be guilty of. Out of the pride of their hearts they have no interest in forgiving others' wrongs done to them; they feel it would be showing weakness to do such a thing. Anger, criticism of others, and faultfinding is their natural course, which they take towards others. It is this habit that binds them and has become the poison toxin that every cell of their being oozes forth. If they are honest with themselves, they must admit that there is no hope for them to find any form of happiness in life. Their hearts have become cold, hardened, embittered, and cruel. They have gouged out the eyes of what could have been a soft, warm heart, and they can no longer see the real way to happiness. They have bound themselves with chains that cannot be broken because of extremely strong bad habits. They have cast themselves into the dark cell of unhappiness for life, with no way to get out, for they do not possess the key of forgiveness and kindness.

At this time the Holiest of all, listening to Nathanael and Patience, and seeing them embracing each other and crying great tears of sorrow for those who, through the pride of their heart, will not take heed to the wise counsel of God, feels their great sorrow. For their hearts are broken on behalf of those who choose to imprison themselves in the dark cell of unhappiness, when all they really need to do is humble themselves before God and take heed to His wise counsel.

Yes, my dear reader, everyone must come to that fork in the road of their own personal adventure called "life." Taking the right road ultimately begins with how we deal with the mistakes of our past.

God shares with Nathanael and Patience that the sole purpose for the rest of their lives will be: to be obedient to the King of Kings and to awaken others by showing them how to live for God's glory and the benefit of others in their own heart. God shares with them that as they depart from this dwelling, in the eyes of all they come to visit with, they will cease to be Nathanael Nobody and Patience. In the hearts' eyes of all in this world of God's creation, they will be "King Time" and "Queen Christian Nature." To each other they will be Nathanael and Patience, but to all others they will be King and Queen. Their purpose will be to use the enchanted powers God will give to them to personally come along side of the citizens of this world and encourage them to live for the glory of God and to be of benefit to each other.

Time and Christian Nature humbly, and in full submission, bow to the true King of all kings. They request that the wisdom and enlightenment that has been given to them will truly be used for God's glory and for the benefit of others, and that they will not abuse the power and authority given to them for their own personal gain. As they both stand and proceed to leave the humble dwelling place of God, they are told by the Holiest of all, what their next adventure is to be. As they depart God's dwelling, they embrace each other tenderly. Christian Nature places her arms around Time's shoulders and as they place their faces close to each other, they proceed to kiss each other with tenderness and affection. They both give thanks to God for: all that He has awakened in them; for the privilege that God has given to them of bringing them together: and desiring to use them for the benefit of all. Even God is emotionally struck with the incredible love that these two have for one another!

Part Three

Somebody Learns His Lesson

Chapter One

The Identity of Time

With newly refreshed hearts Nathanael Nobody and Patience rise early for the purpose of extending a fresh welcome to the dawning of a brand new day. As they exit the dwelling place of God to begin their new adventure in the story of their life, an astonishing change takes place. Patience puts her hands over her mouth as her entire being cries out with a big gasp. Her deep ocean-blue-water eyes now appear to be engulfing her entire face as she cries out, "Nathanael, my forever love, you have changed!" The Nathanael who entered the dwelling of God is not the same Nathanael who has just exited the dwelling of God.

Standing nearly six feet tall, "Time" has now exited the dwelling place of God. The physical appearance of this one, now called "Time," bore no resemblance to the body that entered the presence of God as "Nathanael Nobody." This person was clearly not the same person who had entered. The hair on his head was shining forth a sparkling color of white-silver. Thick and soft as sheep's wool, this hair was parted down the middle and flowed freely down to his shoulders. The color of his face had a reddish-brown appearance that perfectly matched the auburn hair of Patience. The external eyes in the head enclosing his face were enchanted, magical eyes indeed! These eyes were not one color but many colors. These eyes were clear, yet piercing, as if they could look into the very heart of each one he devoted his attention to, clearly reading their very heart. These soft, gentle, caring eyes were unique, indeed! One could see very clearly a blueness as of a skillfully painted sky; a brownness which shined like the sheen on a hand-crafted and loved oaken table; a redness of joy such as one would see on a rosy red apple; a greenness as seen on a specially manicured sports field. Yes, my dear reader, these colors, and many others, could all be seen in these divinely touched, enchanted eyes of the person of Time himself. It was as if Time could clearly see, and fully identify with, every heart that he touched. He could clearly read every heart, as he would look through the eye-gate leading into one's heart. It was as if his eyes were one with whoever his eyes would focus his attention on.

Just as little Evangeline had become a new person many years earlier, as a direct result of sitting and learning at the feet of God for over two thousand years, so Nathanael Nobody has ceased being himself and has become a totally new person after sitting, and quietly learning, at the feet of God. It seems, while in the presence of God, that God had personally entered a very private door into the heart of Nathanael Nobody and given him a new identity. He was now a totally new person, a person who had never actually existed before. A person named "Time" who, with Christian Nature, would now go forth together to nurture, comfort, encourage, and enlighten others to understand the love that God has for them.

For the very first time, this new person named "Time" approaches Christian Nature, embraces her with a deep, tender, affectionate passion, that only two persons in love with each other can comprehend, and reaffirms his love for her. With a loving kiss placed directly upon the lips of this one who will always be the love of his heart, he tenderly expresses his love for her. As nose touches nose and the deep blue-ocean-water eyes of Christian Nature look into the multi-colored eyes of Time, Christian Nature says, "What a wonderful treasure it is when one's forever sweetheart is Time himself."

What a truly enchanting scene this was to see the tender love of Time and Christian Nature together, embracing, holding hands, and devoting themselves to each other. As they lovingly talk to each other, they understand that their sole purpose in life together will be to bring glory to God and happiness and enjoyment into the lives of all whom their lives will now touch.

As the eyes of Christian Nature look deeply into the eyes of Time, Time tells her that each and every time we exit one place in our lives we must realize that we are entering another place to be used by God to encourage others.

Whereas, before they entered the dwelling place of God, it was Christian Nature who was teaching Nathanael Nobody. Now she realizes that it is her love, Time, himself, who has become the primary teacher of her. For this true love of her heart has become a new being as a direct result of sitting and learning at the feet of God. In her heart, she realized that if she will simply listen, there is much that she can learn from Time.

A certain oneness seems to exist between Time and Christian Nature that has never existed between any two persons. It is as if they are two, yet one! Amazing indeed! These two separate persons are one in a common purpose of coming alongside others to bring happiness and enjoyment to each one whom their lives may touch, and to point others to the source of eternal happiness, which is God Himself.

In this magical and enchanted moment, Time calls for Aeromore to show himself. Immediately this little two-inch bird appears and shows himself for who he really is. Suddenly, a massive eagle appears with a wingspan surpassing the distance of more than twenty feet! Each beautifully multi-colored feather of his wings appearing to measure a full twelve inches in length; each sharp talon of his mighty feet reaching nearly a yard in length. Aeromore's tail-feathers fanning out to nearly five yards in width and his razor sharp, six-foot long, beak is able to penetrate any obstacle he approaches with ease. His piercing eyes, carefully and mysteriously disguised within the head of this bald eagle, mysteriously and seemingly in an enchanted manner, sees all things with a keenness of sight and wisdom unmatched by any creature. In the midst of all of the enormous size, strength, and beauty of this magical creature, the heart of this amazing bird continues to tweet in a very humble manner. Filled with the sounds of humility, he sings his sweet little tunes of comfort and encouragement into the multi-colored eyes of Time. Yes, my dear friend, this is the very same bird that tweeted the sweet, inspirational tune Nathanael used to hear when he first met his sweet little insignificant bird in Christian Nature's forest of life. It is truly amazing what God can do with either a person or a creature that has a heart filled with a genuine humility, a humble spirit, and a desire to be a blessing to all whom their lives may touch. God can do mighty things with such a one!

As Evangeline, Nathanael, and Aeromore have all become changed beings as a direct result of the influence of God in their lives, may we all become new created beings as a direct result of God being in our lives. May we all live for the purpose of bringing glory to God and comfort and encouragement to all whom our lives may touch.

Purity of heart and mind is a very difficult quality for any person to achieve in our journey through this vast forest of life. Can mere mortals attain this quality? If we are honest with ourselves, we must say "no," because we have all inherited a sinful human nature and all the ravaging effects that such an incurable disease brings with it. Could it be possible, though, that if one was so full of the Holy Spirit (in our story, filled with the love of the person of Christian Nature), that sinful human nature could be minimized? Could it be possible that a Holy-Spirit-filled person could traverse through the forest of life and bring comfort and encouragement to all whom their life may touch? Such is the case in our story as Time, filled with the Holy Spirit, goes forth, not alone but with Christian Nature, Patience, and the Holy Spirit on their next enchanted adventure.

As Time tenderly embraces Christian Nature, these two persons, consumed with a love for one another and a desire to comfort others, proceed together on their next adventure. It seems that joy follows them in much the same way that a shadow follows its owner. A purity and cleanness, such as one would taste from a source of purified and sparkling fresh cool water, seemed to bubble up from their hearts. As this pure water overflows their hearts, it floods into their minds and consumes them with a joy that seems to follow Time and Christian Nature wherever they go.

The tender, soft, delicacy, and beauty of Christian Nature seems to have such a profound influence on Time that he is consumed with a love for her and a desire to show God's grace to all whom they meet in this journey called "life." As they hold hands in this journey, Christian Nature asks Time, "So what does it mean, my love, to truly live happily?" Time answers, "O my precious one, my true love, to live happily must come from within oneself. It will never come from some outside temporal source. It must come from deep inside one's Holy Spirit-controlled heart! It must come from a heart that has gone through a thorough washing and been scrubbed clean by the personal hand of God Himself; a heart filled with the love of the Holy Spirit; a heart that ventures forth to be a source of encouragement to others," so answered the voice of Time, under the influence of the Holy Spirit, and speaking out of experience.

Time then tells Christian Nature that as they travel throughout all of creation to bring comfort and encouragement to others, they must realize that the only way they can bring beauty to the lives of others is if they will carry it inside themselves. Once again Time looks into the beautiful deep-ocean-blue eyes of Christian Nature, smiles, and tells her how beautiful she is, for she is the most beautiful being of all. He tells her he will treasure her in the deep recesses of his heart all the days of his life.

Time shares with Christian Nature that as each person journeys through life, they must realize that they are like a highly skilled artist in the masterpiece they are painting with their own lives. We all skillfully paint, with the precise paintbrush of our own lives. The material that we use is our own flesh, our own blood – the very marrow in the bones of our own lives. The quality of this work of art, that each person so skillfully produces, is determined by the quality of the painting they make with the material that is given to them.

Time tenderly shares with Christian Nature that each person's life is made up of many, seemingly, small decisions. Each one of these little decisions produces a huge impact on us. Every thought that comes from our heart-controlled mind is a decision. We must always remember the value and see the importance in making decisions that will bring true happiness as a result of demonstrating purity in our hearts, filled with the love of the Holy Spirit.

Time then asks the love of his heart, Christian Nature, what she would do if she knew that she could not fail? Christian Nature answers by saying that she would seek to fill everyone with the kind of love that she has specially devoted to Time. With this, Time once again reaffirms his love for her, that they will always be, forever, in love with each other: two persons, yet one perfect pure love of one man and one woman, forever!

So, our story started with the love of Patience wooing the seemingly blind Nathanael Nobody into beginning to see with the eyes of his blind heart. As he began to see with the eyes of his heart, he began to see many things he had never seen before. He began to see the world that Patience was opening up to the eyes of his heart. He saw the love of his heart, (the Holy Spirit), who had been patiently waiting for him for a very long time. As he was consumed with a love for her, she brought him to Holy God, Himself, who specifically taught him so many things he had never seen the value of before. After being filled with God and being filled with the love of the Holy Spirit, he has now become a totally changed person. Seeing clearly, now as Time, he goes forth to encourage others to be a blessing to all whom their lives may touch. These facts, so real, so amazing, are seldom conveyed to others. But Time asks you to consider these facts of how God may be working in your life as well.

Chapter Two

Journey to a Darkened Heart

Just as old, brown, brittle grass is made new again and given a new life by a simple, gentle rain, so it seems that a renewing visit from God has made Time into the new person he is today. The apostles, in the Bible, became new persons, as a direct result of seeing, with their external eyes, the resurrected Christ. May we all become changed persons as a direct result of seeing, with our heart's eyes, the resurrected Jesus Christ, our personal Savior from our sins. Yes indeed, the thoughts that come from a Holy Spirit-filled heart reawakens us to a fresh excitement that we can all experience, each moment of each day, in our new heart if we will only start each day under the influence of the Holy Spirit in God's Word.

For the very first time, Time and Christian Nature climb onto the back of Aeromore to begin their flight to visit the heart of Somebody. Time tells Aeromore to fly us directly to the land of the heart of Somebody. As Christian Nature, climbs up on Aeromore, directly behind Time, she wraps her loving arms around the waist of Time, places her sweet head on his shoulder and gently kisses his face. As all three begin this flight together, they become magically influenced by the beauty they behold. As they drink in the wonder of getting a bird's-eye view of God's created world of the Christian heart, they behold all the beauty that Christian Nature, (the Holy Spirit) has filled it with. "What a wonderful place to live," Time says to Christian Nature; "In a God-created, Holy Spirit filled heart, where each of its citizens love each other and live for the purpose of bringing comfort and encouragement into the lives of one another."

Time tells Christian Nature, "We need to look at each day in a very singular way. We need to see each day as a separate, one-of-kind creation. To truly receive the full benefit of each day means to seek out that one special moment that each day gives to us as a gift and use that moment to show the love that God wants us to share with some special individual that God puts on our hearts. If God can use us to show His love and eternal life to the heart of one person each day, that's what it means to truly live and experience the joy and the benefit, that the dawning of each new day brings with it."

Before entering the heart-controlled world of Somebody, they journey through the beautiful Christian Nature filled world of a God created heart. Time, Christian Nature, and Aeromore are truly alive; they have refreshed and renewed hearts. Their hearts fully realize the remarkable treasures that are theirs every day.

As the Bible says, in Psalm 90, Time and Christian Nature have come to see the value of numbering their days and seeking to learn all the wisdom they can from each day of their lives. As Time and Christian Nature continue their flight on the back of Aeromore, they reflect on this new authority and power that God has invested in them. Time now has the power to, either, travel or bring the events of the past and future, into the present with no obstacles to prevent such from happening. Christian Nature has the power to do whatever she chooses with the world of Christian Nature. God has invested a large portion of His power in them. It is important that they use it wisely and carefully. Time tells Christian Nature, "In the other world, it seems that most people use extreme force and anger to accomplish what they want to do. To be wise stewards of this power that God has invested in us, we must patiently use the love of the Holy Spirit (as seen in Christian Nature herself), and the wisdom of Time, (shown through the experiences of life itself), to bring the kingdom of the heart of each person we meet into the very presence of God." Christian Nature tells Time, "We should only demonstrate our strength by pulling others up rather than by pushing them down through overpowering strength."

Christian Nature then shares with Time how she seeks to show this truth to others. People in the other world see themselves as hammers, seeking to break other people down by hammering them to pieces. She has sought to use the gentle thaw of Spring to tenderly melt the hardened ice of the winter. In much the same way, gentle words can help melt hardened hearts. A wealth of experience has taught her that the gentle softness of a God-created heart can melt the hardness of a man-made heart. She says that we need to stop doing things the way they do things, in the hardness of the other world. We realize that our actions need to be consistent with dealing with others the same way that our loving God has dealt with us. We need to realize that we now live in the God-created world of a new heart, and the way that we deal with people in our world, our relationships with people, is much more different than the way that people deal with each other in the other world.

Both Time and Christian Nature fully understand that their power needs to be used to do good things for other people, rather than using their God-given power to exert the force of a wrongly used power on others.

What a wonderful adventure in God's created world this has been. As they exit God's beautiful world of a Christian Nature filled, Holy Spirit filled heart, they now enter a world of darkness. A dark, cold, gloomy world, in the kingdom of the heart of Somebody the Great, now awaits them!

Chapter Three

Time and Christian Nature Meet Somebody

The depressive, dark, and gloomy heart of Stephan Somebody the Great proves to be the destination of the next God appointed adventure for Time and Christian Nature. As Aeromore lands in the kingdom of the heart of Somebody, Time and Christian Nature dismount and find themselves touching ground in what appears to be a damp swamp-like surrounding. Before them stands a castle, one hundred feet tall reaching towards a sky of overcast, dismal gray coloring. The castle walls are made of ten-foot thick bricks of solid gold bars, nearly seventy feet high. These golden bricks surround the castle itself, which is made of sparkling diamonds. It appears that the resident of this fortress has a love for what he considers great wealth, in this fortification that he has made for himself in his heart. This castle seems to scream to all, "Stay away from me, for I am better than you!"

As Time and Christian Nature study the external appearance of this architecture of human pomposity, they wonder what kind of a proud, arrogant creature lives here. From within the confines of this man-made fortress of supposed financial success, a voice cries out, "Go away! I have no need for anybody!" The voice of Stephan Somebody says, "My devoted evil slaves have told me rumors of the two of you. I should have known God would send you here."

Time tells Christian Nature that it appears that a true adventure awaits them in this place. He says, "Somebody has spent a lot of his time in an effort to be very bad. If we can get him to spend an equal amount of his time in being good, maybe he won't be so bad anymore!" Goodness can only come from a heart that is filled with the love of the Holy Spirit. Hence, Time and Christian Nature have a true adventure standing before them!

Time calls to Somebody and tells him that they desire to enter his man-made fortress. Somebody answers, "Go away! I have no need of you. I am the biggest, strongest, and wealthiest of all. Go away, lest I overpower you!" With this Christian Nature places the open palm of her right hand to her lips and very gently blows a breath of fresh wind in the direction of Somebody's mighty structure. Immediately his solid gold walls come tumbling down and Stephan Somebody stands in the presence of Time and Christian Nature. As Time and Christian Nature, for the first time, look into the kingdom of the heart of Somebody, they see a strange sight. This one, who wants others to think he is a big man, stands nearly, but not quite, five feet tall. This toxic five-foot monstrosity of human pride has a body that fills the air with the foul odor of evil thoughts. His foul odor seems to emit a vapor of toxic waste. It cries out the story of the wrongs that he has committed towards others in how he accumulated his wealth, prestige, and the power he holds over those who follow him. His personal slaves, who are all around him, seem to be bent over as if the verbal abuse, that he has constantly hurled upon them, has placed a heavy burden upon their back.

As Time and Christian Nature view this scene, Time tells Christian Nature, "It's always been a mystery to me to see that some people take great honor in humiliating other people. It appears that this little man's greed for financial gain has so consumed his life, that he really has no life at all. He has paid a very high price, in the cost of his life, for the valuable time he has used to accumulate this supposed wealth."

An astonished Somebody glares at Christian Nature and says, "What have you done, woman, to my precious walls of gold? No matter, I love my gold! I love my silver! I love my great financial abundance! I do not understand you two insignificant creatures. Why do you not bow before me as everyone else does? Do you not understand the financial worth of the person before whom you now stand? I am Stephan Somebody the Great! I am the king in the kingdom of this heart into which you have entered without being invited."

Time responds to Somebody's proud boast by saying, "We are Time and Christian Nature. We serve God, the King of all kings. We have been sent by the Holy God, Himself, to teach you the most valuable lesson you may ever learn."

To this, Somebody responds by saying, "At one time I trusted this King of kings, this God whom you serve. I trusted him as my Savior from sin. But I trust Him no more. I trust no one now but myself! I am the king of my heart! I rule and reign in my heart! I have deposed your King from my throne and I reign supreme! I put all my hope and confidence in my gold! I rejoice now, for my financial wealth is very great! My wicked slaves have told me that you two would eventually come to my kingdom. I have no time to waste with Time, and I have no patience to let the Holy Spirit move in my heart by showing me herself through the heart of Christian Nature."

Christian Nature whispers to Time that apparently this evil-eyed creature, who devotes his life to accumulating financial wealth, has not considered the poverty that is sure to come upon him. Christian Nature shares with Time the sorrow she feels in her Holy Spirit filled heart over the darkened heart in the kingdom in which this small creature lives. They both come to understand that at one time, God was his King. Now, however, he only sees, hears, and feels with his external eyes, ears, and hands. He has locked God out of his heart, which previously had been bought with the blood of God Himself. Such is the state of the heart that has blinded itself to the beauty that God had previously shown to him. Yes, my dear reader, such is the heart of one who has turned away from God and has become hardened through an all-consuming, darkened financial greed!

Christian Nature tells Time, "We must use the power God has given to us to bring this person back to God." Time addresses Somebody by saying, "Time has come for you to learn from the mistakes you have made in your past. Time has brought with us your personal instructors, your mistakes, to teach you eternal truth." "I have made no mistakes!" says Somebody. "Then tell me, Somebody, who are all of these instructors and teachers, yes, this vast multitude of teachers who now stand before us?" With this, seemingly out of nowhere, many teachers appear from Somebody's past life. Yes, my dear reader, Time has used his God-given authority to bring out of the past Somebody's mistakes, and magically turned them into enchanted teachers, in the present, to teach this wayward saint some valuable lessons. "What magic is this?" shouts Somebody. To this, the multi-colored, deep-piercing eyes of Time solemnly and seriously look into the cold dark eyes of Somebody and says, "It is time for your instructors to enlighten you to what you already know to be true."

With this said, the first instructor of his past mistakes walks up to him, snaps his fingers in the face of Somebody and immediately they are in Somebody's youth. The setting is a church service. The beautiful Patience of the Holy Spirit of God has convictingly moved on the heart of young Stephan to see his own personal sin and the incredible love that Jesus Christ has for him by dying for his sins on the Cross. With heart breaking repentance and remorse, young Stephan repents of his sin, and with a newly God-created heart, he asks Jesus to be the King of his heart and Savior from his sin. It seems that young Stephan is like a new person. As Queen Christian Nature fills his heart with the beautiful world of Christian Nature, he is truly happy! He is happy because he can now see, hear, and feel new things in his heart, things that young Stephan had never seen, heard, or felt before. What a wonderful day this was! As this instructor from his past gently looks into the now cold, dark eyes of Stephan Somebody, he teaches him an important lesson by saying, "Never forget, Stephan, that Jesus Christ has always loved you. He loves you today! It is as if only you, and you alone, matter to Him. His only desire is for you to humble yourself, acknowledge your sinfulness, and come running back into the loving embrace of the all-forgiving Savior of your heart!"

As this instructor magically disappears at the snap of Time's fingers, Somebody screams, "Foolishness! I was an ignorant, foolish child, easily manipulated by the cunning craftiness of an over zealous preacher seeking to manipulate my mind for his own personal gain. Foolishness indeed! I will have no more of that!"

As Somebody seeks to walk away, Christian Nature snaps her fingers and immediately roots spring forth from under his feet and securely fasten his feet to the ground. Yes indeed, my dear reader, Christian Nature herself produces a magically Time-enchanted plot of soil underneath the feet of Somebody, and securely fastened his feet to this soil upon which he stands. Amazingly, in this dark, cold, gloomy land of Somebody's heart, this one small plot of soil has been claimed by the wisdom of Time, enchanted by the power of Christian Nature, and securely holds Somebody by the mysterious God-granted magical power of these two servants of God. "What is this magic? Let me go," screams Somebody! To this, Time and Christian Nature say nothing. But their penetrating eyes look deep into Somebody's cold dark eyes and together these two snap their fingers and instructor number two magically appears.

When instructor number two appears before Somebody, he, then, snaps his fingers. The scene is in a church service. Young Stephan, though he is in church, his mind is elsewhere. His mind is consumed with the stories he has been absorbing about the great financial millionaires and the methods they used to accumulate their great wealth. They are famous, successful, and prosperous. Everyone bows to them, worships them, and seeks their autographs. "I want to be rich," young Stephan says to himself. "But how can I get started?" With this he sees the offering plate come by filled to overflowing with the financial freewill offerings of others giving to God in thankfulness for what God has given to them. An idea pops into Stephan's head. While no one is looking he unloads the contents of the offering plate, and fills his own pockets with its contents. He slyly smiles to himself and says, "Now I will start to become rich!" The next day, this greedy, selfish young man, who no longer looks at anything with the eyes of his God-created heart, but only looks at all things with his greedy, external, temporary eyes, only sees what his sinful human nature now attractively shows him. He has locked the door to his God-created heart, thrown away the key and now cobwebs begin to form before this door. The poisonous spiders of his sinful human nature have now completely blinded him to the beauty of Christian Nature, so much so, that he can no longer see the beauty that God had for him.

Somebody screams, "O yes, the beginning of my financial literacy, my road to success. It all started with the offering plate. Hooray for me!"

With tears in the eyes of instructor number two, he turns to Time and Christian Nature as Time snaps his fingers and instructor number two disappears. With tears forming in the eyes of Time and Christian Nature, Time silently snaps his fingers and instructor number three appears. With a look of humility on his face, he walks up to Somebody and snaps his fingers. Immediately the scenes are shown of how Stephan became a great man of wealth: by taking from others small investments and making great financial wealth with it to benefit only himself. Through the sly, cunning, and deceptive ways of "leverage," he had discovered how to bring financial wealth to himself by making small investments in others, and then making them his slaves for life. He used them to fill his pockets with golden coins of supposed financial happiness.

Yes, through the sly, cunning, deceptive ways of a wrongly used financial literacy, young Stephan had become "The Great Stephan Somebody" he had craved to be. He was a success! He knew how to manipulate and play the Wall Street financial markets for his own gain. He knew how to successfully purchase precious metals, particularly gold, which his life had become defined by. The massive walls around his castle of diamonds were ascending to unprecedented heights with solid golden slabs, each one individually printed with his own image. Stephan had become Somebody! God, who gave His life for him on the cross of Calvary, had become nobody to him. Somebody was a success! People now flocked to him in the other world for his great financial wisdom of how to become successful in building financial wealth. He was writing best selling books that were flying off the shelves. Yes, indeed, this man was successful! He was constantly signing autographs. He had arrived! He was the role model for all aspiring students of financial wealth building. As instructor number three disappears with the snapping of Time's fingers, the eyes of the hearts of Time and Christian Nature are clearly broken as great rivers of sorrowing tears form in the presence of Stephan Somebody the Great.

To this Somebody cries out, "What are you crying about? I am a success story! I have achieved what few have ever achieved! I can go nowhere without autograph seekers surrounding me!" Christian Nature snaps her fingers and immediately his arms are stretched out and securely fastened by magically appearing trees, which seem to fasten his hands to their rugged bark. Stephan Somebody can no longer move. His feet are securely fastened to the ground. His arms are stretched out and securely fastened by their hands to seemingly magical trees. His sinful past has so secured him that he is bound by his past with chains. He can no longer move, but he believes he is a success! This "successful" Somebody can no longer move because he has so become bound with the financial chains of success in the other world.

Time silently snaps his fingers and instructor number four, from the past, magically appears. Instructor number four reveals the atrocious crimes against others that Somebody has committed in order to increase his already massive financial fortune. Scenes are shown of him foreclosing and taking away the homes of people. These people were doing all they could; they were working hard to make ends meet. They had little money through their low-paying jobs and they could not make their monthly expenses. Somebody took away their homes, which he justified by saying they belonged to him. He rented them to others, and the cycle would continue.

Somebody, through the manipulation of naive stock investors, successfully mastered the skill of taking their money and giving them no return on their investments. Yes, indeed, through these, and many other "successful" financial schemes, Somebody had become a financial success! As instructor number four revealed many of these scenes for all to see, Time and Christian Nature were sobbing, almost uncontrollably. They understood the potential that Somebody's God-created heart could have provided for him; the beauty of a heart filled with love, goodness, kindness, and gentleness by Christian Nature. Time and Christian Nature fully understood the wonderful, loving people whom he could have met in his God-created heart. The God-given wisdom that had been given through the experiences of life to Time, and the beauty of living the Holy Spirit-filled, Christian Nature-filled lifestyle of what could have happened in Somebody's heart, caused extreme sorrow for Time and Christian Nature.

As Christian Nature snaps her fingers, instructor number four, vanishes. Immediately thorns appear and hammer themselves into the immovable hands and feet of Somebody. The crowning achievement of his "successful" life is a crown of thorns, painfully embedded upon the "successful" brain of his life.

King Time and Queen Christian Nature slowly walk up to the immovable Somebody and place their faces right up to his immovable face. The multi-colored eyes of Time, which can see clearly into the hardest of hearts, look into, and read, the very heart of his soul. The blue-ocean-water eyes of Christian Nature, which possess the convicting power of the Holy Spirit, are now filled to overflowing with tears. Both King Time and Queen Christian Nature can hardly speak as their quaking crying words whisper in a sorrowful manner, "Are you truly happy Mr. Somebody? You are bound by the sins of your life. Are you now feeling the awful pain of the thorn-produced nails that are hurting you so badly? Your sins have caused the same pain to the Holy God. Because God loves you so much, He died for your sins; He suffered this pain and agony for your sins, Mr. Somebody. He died for you, Mr. Somebody!"

Queen Christian Nature then speaks and says with the full force of her convicting power of the Holy Spirit, "Please repent of your sins, Mr. Somebody, and become Nobody!" Time, who is really a Nobody, then says, "Are you really happy, Mr. Somebody?"

Chapter Four

The Repentance of Somebody

In much the same way that the warmness of heat coming from the sun melts the cold, brutal, hardness of a frozen glacier, so the supernatural convicting power of the Holy Spirit of God has melted the cold, hardened heart of Stephan Somebody the Great. Shown so beautifully in the Patience of Christian Nature, this warm, melting conviction from the Holy Spirit has had a remarkable impact upon the kingdom within the heart of this wayward saint. In response to the convicting words of the Holy Spirit and the wise experience of Time, Somebody melts, like ice on a hot August sidewalk, and begins sobbing great tears of grief. Even though Somebody had become a financial success in the other world, he felt no happiness at all in the deep recesses of his heart. In his heart, he was extremely uncomfortable. He felt completely alone. Inside his heart, if truth were told, he was freezing cold. He had never experienced the warmth that only comes from being surrounded by warm, loving Christians who are filled with the love of the Holy Spirit; those who are sharing the patient beauty of Christian Nature with those around them.

Yes, my dear reader, "The Great Stephan Somebody" was not comfortable with himself at all! He was cold and felt all alone in his successful heart. He had found that his successful heart began to hate his achievements. The sour and dishonest methods used to attain his financial success were now sickening to him. He learned that, if one does not have someone to share financial wealth with, then one will never find delight in having it.

Yes, my dear reader, as the wise voice of experience, through Time himself, speaks to his heart, Somebody comes to understand that if he really wants to be happy, he really doesn't need to have any more financial wealth than he truly needs. If he really wants to become wise, he needs to start by: being honest with himself; stop expressing the desires of a darkened man-made heart; and stop playing the fool! He needs to stop being proud, pretending to know it all, and admit that he knows nothing with regard to what has real worth and value.

Somebody comes to understand, through the wise teaching of Time, that it is as if he were born yesterday; he really doesn't know anything at all! Time had taught him that his endless words of pride and arrogance (which were coming from his man-made heart), were like the wind, they were endless. He was multiplying these words at an endless rate, and they contained absolutely no real knowledge of truth in them at all (Job 38). The wisdom of the experience of Time taught him that, though he thought he was wise, he knew he was a fool. Through the wisdom of the experience of Time, and through the Patience of the convicting power of the Holy Spirit, seen in the beauty of Christian Nature, Somebody came to understand the sinfulness of his ways. He came to understand the horrors that would come upon him if he continued living his life in this manner. He came to understand that it was his proud and arrogant heart that had brought him to this place. He came to understand how little of true worth he really knows; that he actually knew nothing at all!

Stephan Somebody, then, does something that he had not done in years. He begins to cry; he begins to sob great rivers of grief and sorrow. With a heart that begins to melt, as the great polar ice caps, his proud melting heart forms great rivers of sorrow over his sinful ways. Stephan Somebody, through a genuine repentance over his sinful life and a sincere humility, begins to show the first signs of wisdom. Yes, Stephan Somebody, in the full sight of the experience of Time, and in the presence of the Holy Spirit, humbles himself. He sincerely seeks God's forgiveness and asks that God, through Patience, would give to him the beauty that Christian Nature has to offer. Through doing so, he receives from God Himself, through the Holy Spirit, the gifts of God's grace and God's forgiveness.

Stephan Somebody comes to understand that the wealth of eternal life, found only in investing his insignificant life in Jesus Christ, and having a desire to please Him, is more important and valuable than the sterile, cold world of supposed financial success. Only in giving one's life, as a living sacrifice to Jesus Christ, can one find a true life worth living! He came to understand that through the wisdom of experience in Time, God always has his unique ways of humbling those who exalt themselves. God, ironically, has a strange way of lifting those up who truly, and with a sincere heart, humble themselves, acknowledge their sins, and ask God to forgive them of their sinful ways. Somebody came to see the importance of exalting only God with his life and not his own proud and arrogant accumulation of supposed worldly success. He came to see, clearly, from the newly awakened eyes in his heart, the many curses that come to the heart filled with pride. He gave a half smile and said, "The mistakes of my life have taught me a hard lesson about the importance and the value of sincere humility. My proud heart has been such a waste of my time and has cost me dearly in the pursuits of my life!"

The voice of Time speaks to him and tells him that because he has truly humbled himself, and has sought God's forgiveness for his sinful ways, he has graciously received God's forgiveness. God will lift him up!

The Holy Spirit, in the beautiful form of Christian Nature, now begins to miraculously change the kingdom of the heart of Stephan Somebody. No longer is it a dark, gloomy, gray, dismal, and swamp-like kingdom of the heart. The gold, diamonds, and financial wealth have been exchanged for the wealth of a heart filled with the beauty that only Christian Nature can provide. As the thorns magically disappear from Stephan's hands and feet, and the crown of thorns from his head, so do the roots holding his feet and the branches securing his arms.

As Stephan drops to his knees and covers his face with his hands, he is uncontrollably weeping. He has come to understand the incredible pain and suffering that Jesus Christ endured on the Cross for his sins. Yes, he weeps uncontrollably over the pain and sorrow that he has willfully inflicted on the Lord and Savior of his unworthy soul, that being Jesus Christ. "How can God ever forgive me of my sins?" he cries out. "I am so very sorry. O God, I beg of you to please forgive me!"

In this enormous emotional moment, the Holy Spirit comes next to him, and Queen Christian Nature comforts him with the beauty found only in Patience and the ministry of the Holy Spirit. The wisdom of the voice of experience, as seen in Time, puts his hand on the shoulder of Stephan and says, "Time has much to show you in your life that is still in your future. In Time, I will show you these wonderful things. The Holy God has some wonderful things He wants to do in you, and through you, to bring glory to God and benefit to all whom your life may touch. No one else can do this, only you! Yes, Stephan, there are wonderful and marvelous things that God will do through you. I will soon take you into the future and let you get a glimpse of how God will use you to help others in a way that only you can do." Stephan responds by saying, "I am so unworthy. I am so undeserving of God using me at all. I have been so sinful. I don't deserve God's blessing of using me at all. I have been so sinful!" Time and Christian Nature look at each other, smile, and together they say to Stephan, "It is because you are honest with yourself that God will use you in a way you have never imagined."

With teary eyes, Time and Christian Nature, now kneeling down on each side of Stephan, lovingly look at each other and softly blow a kiss to each other. They both know, by experience, the unique ways in which God can use those who are honest with themselves about who they really are.

As this great change takes place within the kingdom of the heart of Stephan, a wonderful magic takes place. The beauty of the Christian Nature makes all things beautiful in the kingdom in the heart of Stephan. The dismal gray sky is now transformed into a beautiful, sunny blue sky. The previous bare skeleton-like trees now begin to flourish with delicious fruit to freely give to the now freed slaves in the kingdom of the heart of Stephan. The previous dry, brown meadows that had been so brittle are now flourishing and prospering with a healthy greenness for the enjoyment of all. Flowers now appear where, before, there had only been thorns. Charming birds sing their melodious melodies of happiness, where before there had only been scavenging vultures who were preying on the misfortunes of others. Yes, my dear friends, as Stephan sees this great miracle that God brings about in the revived and renewed heart of a wayward saint, he rejoices and gives thanks to God for His wonderful amazing grace!!!

Chapter Five

Stephan's New Heart

What a truly remarkable shower of God's blessings poured down upon the heart of the new Stephan! As each of us experience the cleanness and renewing freshness that a cleansing shower gives, in much the same way, Stephan received this grace-gift from God. We have all experienced the uncomfortable feeling of being dirty, grimy, sweaty, sticky, smelly, and just plain filthy as a result of the influences that each day can produce on us. Each fleshy pore of the cells of our sinful human nature produces a stinking filthiness that actually does cause our entire physical being to be uncomfortably filthy. As we go through the cleansing, renewing, and refreshing experience of a shower, we are made clean by soap and water. We feel like new again! Such is the case with Stephan. The filthy ugliness of totally enjoying wallowing around in the personal surroundings (created by himself in his own heart) has made him feel miserable. He smelled horrible as each and every cell of his being was wretchedly filthy and oozed forth the odor of the toxic waste produced by his life. It has all changed now!

By God's Grace he has voluntarily stepped into the cleansing, renewing shower of God's blessings! This previously hardened heart, though God had truly redeemed it in his youth, was softened, cleansed, and renewed, again, by God. The fresh, soft soap of the Holy Spirit, in great detail, scrubbed clean each nook and cranny of his heart. The washing of the pure, clean water of the Holy Spirit washed away all the filthiness of sin that his uncontrolled, sinful nature had consumed his heart with. It was as if he were a new person, clean, renewed, refreshed, and revived just to experience all the wonders of what God desires to awaken in him.

A new enchanted magic is now performed by the work of the Holy Spirit, through Patience, and the wonder of Christian Nature. Christian Nature reveals a special key. With this key, she slowly opens the door of Stephan's previously locked and bolted-shut hard heart. As Stephan, Christian Nature, and Time look into the newly opened door of Stephan's heart, they see true magic indeed! It is as if a special enchantment has been placed upon Stephan's heart, and the Holy Spirit, through the Patience of the hands of Christian Nature, has consumed his heart with beauty everywhere. What had previously been so dark, filthy, and ugly, was now a beautiful heart.

Queen Christian Nature has filled his heart with the beauty of the Holy Spirit, as seen in Christian Nature. In much the same way that Christian Nature started filling God's created world after immediately being taught by God for over two thousand years, so she now goes about in Stephan's heart, filling it with the exquisite beauty that only the Holy Spirit can do, in the form of Christian Nature.

As Time, Christian Nature, and Stephan walk around in his new heart, Stephan is truly astonished. A smile as large as a dinner plate covers his entire face as he is filled with joy over what the Holy Spirit has done in his heart. The beauty of the trees, the refreshing dew and coolness of the mornings, the fragrance of the beautiful flowers, the pleasantness and sweetness afforded by the grass of the meadows, and the soul-enriching purity of clean air. All of these treasures are so wonderful, so delightful, so intoxicating to the heart of one who had not experienced this for a long time! All of this made possible by God's amazing grace!

So it is for the newly revived Christian, who has been restored and renewed to the beauty of having a new relationship with God. As a result of humbling himself he receives the cleansing shower of God's forgiveness!

Stephan drops to his knees, with hands over his face and sobs great tears of happiness. "I am so undeserving of all of this. I do not deserve this beautiful heart. I do not feel worthy of living in such a beautiful place that only God can create. I am truly unworthy and undeserving of all this," cries Stephan.

The wisdom found in the experience of Time, now tells Stephan that, "Time and Christian Nature are now here to take you to visit with God, Himself." "How can I do such a thing! I am the most undeserving and unworthy of all humans who have ever walked this earth. I just want to spend the rest of my life thanking God and expressing my gratitude for what God has done for me. To actually visit God Himself, I cannot do it. I feel so unworthy, so undeserving!"

"It is very good for you to feel this way," says the experience and wisdom of Time. "However, you must know that God is only beginning to speak to your heart. There are many, never-imagined things that God plans on doing in your Christian-Nature-filled-heart that you never thought possible. God has given Christian Nature and myself the privilege of actually bringing you to Him. Once with God, He will fully open the eyes of your heart to see clearly the beauty of this wonderful new life that He has made available to you in your heart. Yes, indeed, my dear friend, you will find yourself becoming someone who you never thought possible. You will be used by God to bring happiness, joy, and comfort to everyone who your life will touch. Your purpose will now be to live to God's glory, to bring joy to others, and to be a comfort to all whom your life may touch."

"O that such a thing could be! How can this all happen?" cries Stephan. Time and Christian Nature just smile at each other, and with a twinkle in their eye they say, "God has His unique ways of making each one of us a totally new person. He has His way of doing things in us, and through us, that we never dreamed could ever happen. It all takes place in our Christian-Nature-filled-heart, Stephan. Through Patience, the Holy Spirit fills your heart with the beauty of Christian Nature! Imagine living in the real God-created heart in the world of your imagination. There is no limit to what God can do in it, and through it, to bring glory to God and to be a benefit to others."

With all this said, Time mounts Aeromore, Christian Nature climbs on immediately behind Time, and Stephan climbs on behind Christian Nature. As Nature wraps her loving arms around the chest of her sweetheart, Time, and cradles her head on the side of his neck, she kisses his cheek and whispers something sweet into his ear. Time silently smiles at her and kisses her and streams of happy tears flow down their cheeks.

As Aeromore begins his flight, they fly over the new kingdom in the heart of Stephan. As Stephan begins to comprehend the beauty in his God-created heart, he endlessly, and constantly, is praising and giving thanks to God. As Time and Christian Nature listen to these sweet sounds, they rejoice, for they both know that their own God-created hearts have uttered the same sounds.

Stephan says, "May I never be called "Somebody" ever again! How I wish I had a different name! I am now, by God's grace, a different person. I wish I had the name of "Nobody." For I am Nobody, an unimportant person. Certainly no one of significance!"

To this Time and Christian Nature look each other in the eye, smile, and then Time says, "So, you want to call yourself 'Nobody.' That's a good and proper name indeed! I once knew someone named 'Nobody.' A sinful man indeed, but God cleaned his heart also and gave him a new heart and new name and he doesn't exist anymore." "That's too bad," says Stephan, "for I would really like to meet this one named 'Nobody.' I would consider it a great privilege to embrace him and call him my brother, all because of the new heart that God has given to both of us."

Christian Nature, looking into the eyes of Time says, "Stephan, 'Nobody' still exists. He is closer to you, right now, than you could ever imagine. It was God who gave him a new name, and the power and authority to come alongside others. With the Holy Spirit, he now teaches the wisdom of experience that comes through Time. Yes, Stephan, 'Nobody' is real. He still exists. He will always be who he is, he is 'Nobody,' and some day God may give you the privilege of meeting him!" Time, with Christian Nature lovingly cradled on the side of his neck, silently smiles at her and kisses her. Time then says, "It is true Stephan. 'Nobody' will always be 'Nobody' no matter who others may think he may be!"

To all this Stephan says, "I sure would like to meet this one named 'Nobody!' I feel that I already know him. I feel that our hearts are beating together as one. It seems we both live for the common purpose of giving glory to God and being a source of comfort and encouragement to others. I would really like to meet 'Mr. Nobody,' for I am 'Nobody' too! Do you think I will ever meet him?" "I do Stephan. I believe you will meet him, indeed!" says Time.

Chapter Six

Stephan's Camp Meeting with God

As Aeromore lands in the place chosen by God, Time, Christian Nature, and Stephan stand in awe and astonishment at the designated meeting place that Stephan will personally share with the Holiest of all. Whereas, Nathanael Nobody was hand-fed by God in the midst of a beautiful forest, and specifically, in the presence of a one-thousand-foot-circumference mighty redwood tree, Stephan will be taught by God in a totally different environment. Yes, my dear reader, as Stephan dismounts Aeromore, he is met by the Ahira Nathtali who tells Stephan to follow him as he leads Stephan to God. "What is this we are walking on?" says Stephan to Ahira. Ahira replies, "This is the sawdust trail. This is all that remains of your old, proud, arrogant heart. It has been sawed into dust by the convicting power of the Holy Spirit, and through the wise experience of Time, who have both worked diligently on your old proud heart, to make it the sawdust it is today. As humility overcomes pride, God desires you to now come to Him in your new, soft, poor, humble heart by walking on the remains of your sawed up old proud heart."

With the eyes of his heart freely flowing tears, Stephan walks the sawdust trail to come into the presence of God. As they come to the entrance of God's dwelling, Ahira tells him to enter God's presence alone, and Ahira departs.

What does this dwelling place of God's own choosing look like, you may ask? Unique indeed! Encompassing an area of more than ten thousand square feet, many people could gather into this seemingly massive-sized tent. Even though many hearts could gather here, it seemed there was only room for the heart of Stephan and God. Stephan had been told earlier to not look at the face of God, but to drop to his knees with his face to the ground. For one is not to look into the face of God. As Stephan does this, the scene is truly a thing of beauty, and a joy to be treasured forever. For you see, my dear reader, "Stephan Somebody the Great," the great financial success, the proud arrogant millionaire in the other world, has truly become a new person.

Stephan cries out, "O Holy One, I am so undeserving of your grace. I am nobody! I am nothing! A person of no significance! Thank you, so very much, for forgiving me of all of my horrible sins. There have been so very many. I am so undeserving of the least of all of your mercy to me! I know nothing but the experience of your heart-saving grace. Please teach me and show me what you would do with my insignificant life."

Stephan comes to see that his life from this point on will be used by God, will be spent by God, to invest in a purpose that will outlive his life. The quality that God will produce through his life will bring great joy to millions of people. He will become a true artist in the artwork of joy that God will do through his life benefiting others. He begins to learn and understand the wisdom that the value of his mistakes of his past life have taught him. He sees that his past life has seemingly been defined by mistakes. Now he must use the wisdom gained from the past experience of his mistakes to continually grow at a rate that he will learn from the wisdom that God will give to him. Just as God has forgiven him, at all times, he must have the sincere desire to forgive others the wrongs done to him. He needs to keep his heart always soft and forgiving. In every corner of his heart, may it constantly be filled with thankfulness and gratitude to God and to others for all that they have done to benefit him. He needs to consider the contents of his heart like a plate filled with three different courses of highly nutritious, healthy, spiritual food that he will have the privilege to indulge in every day. The first course that he should partake of is the freshness of forgiveness. Like picking fresh vegetables that are so good for his physical body, pick the fresh vegetables of forgiveness from the garden in his heart. No matter what others have done for you, always forgive! The second course that he needs to feed on each day is the seasoned delicacy of thankfulness and gratitude, which will enhance his life with health benefits he never imagined. He comes to see that his heart is full of thankfulness to others. It is like being filled with the rich protein that his spiritual body needs so desperately to sustain him through the rigors of life. The third course, the finishing course of his daily meal, is to fill up his plate and indulge himself with all the fruits of kindness that he can possibly eat. He sees the importance, the imperativeness, of filling himself up to overflowing with the sweet taste of this highly nutritious fruit. He sees that to truly show kindness in all that he does is much more important than any form of wisdom. As a matter of fact, to show kindness to others, to take advantage of every opportunity to show kindness, is the first step to truly becoming wise! If a person chooses not to be kind to others as a lifestyle practice, there is absolutely no way of that person becoming wise no matter how much they think they know about life. Stephan sees that it is important, it is imperative, for him to place himself at this dinner table and partake by indulging in this three course meal each and every day of his life. He needs to develop the practice of making it a habit, a daily habit, so strong that the chains of it can never be broken.

"O God," Stephan cries out, "You have filled me with the everlasting wisdom of your eternal truth. How I am so unworthy and undeserving of being taught by You these wonderful truths. Please help me to never forget them, to treasure them, and to apply them, everyday, in my life."

God then shares with Stephan that the sweet Holy Spirit will live in his heart in much the same way the Holy Spirit lives in the heart of Nathanael Nobody. He realizes that the Holy Spirit, through beautiful Patience, will fill his heart with the enchanted magic that only Queen Christian Nature herself can bring about in a heart totally given over to God.

Stephan, in a state of happiness upon hearing the name of Nathanael Nobody, reacts with an emotional excitement. For the story of Nathanael Nobody has spread far and wide in this enchanted land of the heart. He was the one who could only see the reality of this land when the famed Patience, Queen Christian Nature herself, through the Holy Spirit, gently moved on his heart to begin to see all things with the eyes of his heart. Yes, when Nathanael Nobody first arrived in this land, he did not know who he really was. It was not until the beautiful Patience took him to meet God that he came to understand the person he really was, and came to see how God would use him, in a way never seen before, to bring glory to God and benefit to others, in being "Time," himself.

Stephan comes to understand that it was his role model, Nathanael Nobody, King Time, who, along with Queen Christian Nature, who had come along side of him and were used by God to totally change his life. It was the wonderful filling of the Holy Spirit, through Queen Christian Nature, who had filled the real world of his heart with the reality of what it means to truly live out of our heart, the beauty of the Christian life. All of this for the purpose of bringing glory to God and comfort and encouragement into the lives of others!

As God instructs Stephan in the specifics of who he will now be, and of how God will use him, he kneels in awe and wonderment, and cries great tears of happiness over how God can use one who has a heart filled with the Patience and beauty of Queen Christian Nature.

As Stephan walks back on the sawdust trail that lead to such a revival in his new heart, he leaps with joy over the amazing things of what God can do in a life. As he exits Gods tent of a renewed covenant with him, he immediately sees Time and Christian Nature. He gives thanks to Queen Christian Nature for the Patience of beauty which she, by the Holy Spirit, has filled his heart with. He shakes hands with Time and says, "I have so desired to meet you Mr. Nobody! You have been my role model all along! You are the real Nathanael Nobody! How I have longed to meet you! Permit me to introduce myself. I am your brother, Nicholaus Nobody!!!"

Chapter Seven

Stephan's New Identity and Adventure

Until the time comes when we are actually escorted into heaven, there is no sweeter fellowship that Christians can enjoy than the fellowship with one another. It is as if there would be a group of Christians gathering together and the only possession they would have would be one simple, small loaf of bread. As they break it and share it with each other, a magical enchantment takes place in that one small loaf of bread, which saturates each heavenly-touched morsel, touched by the finger of God. As these fellowshipping saints consume this treasure of God's provision, it would seem it would all be eaten. In its place though, a new loaf magically appears for each to enjoy fellowship around. Such is the case when Christians enjoy sweet fellowship with other Christians, and the sweetness never ends! Such fellowship never lacks for provision and enjoyment in all that God has to offer.

The fellowship of the brothers Nobody, Nathanael and Nicholaus, combined with the beautiful Patience of Christian Nature, all filled with the Holy Spirit, was truly a sight to behold. This sight was one that could only be seen in a God-created heart, and with the eyes of a heart filled with the wonderment of our imagination! What fellowship indeed! A treasure that belongs to God, for He has purchased these hearts with the cost of His own blood!

These three humans are no longer who they once were. They are now three new creations of God, with new identities. Each one being used by God in a never-before-seen unique way to bring glory to God and encouragement, comfort, and joy into the lives of all whom their lives may touch. Evangeline was changed by God into "Queen Christian Nature," and through Patience and the Holy Spirit, is filling hearts with the beauty of Christian Nature. Nathanael Nobody, seldom looked at anything with the eyes of his heart, until the lovely Patience began wooing him to God and opened the eyes of his heart, by the Holy Spirit, to see the incredible beauty of Queen Christian Nature. He came to see all that the Holy Spirit can do with a heart filled with such a Christian Nature. Now, in his new identity as "Time," he goes about with free access to the past, present, and future to, along with Christian Nature, teach others what only Time can teach. Stephan Somebody, previously possessed with a heart filled with arrogance and pride over his financial success and fame, is now a truly humble heart, "Nicholaus Nobody," with a desire to take all of his financial wealth and freely give it away to help others with their financial needs. Yes, indeed, my dear friends, these three true-to-life saints are three separate persons, yet with one common desire: to bring glory to God and benefit to others. When these three saints are together, the fellowship of Time, Christian Nature, and Saint Nicholaus is grand indeed!

The new "Saint Nicholaus" now shares with Time and Christian Nature the adventure God has given to him. Unlike Time and Christian Nature, his adventure will be in the other world. Both Time and Christian Nature put their hands over their mouths and let out a collective gasp of fear! Time says, "My dear brother, the inhabitants of that world are cruel, cold, and brutal. Their hearts are full of evil intent. They will probably try to do you great harm. They take great pride in hurting others. I know, for I once lived in the country of such hearts!" "Nevertheless," Nicholaus says, "I will go. I will love these people and constantly give to them the joyous gifts of God's love in the hope of someday bringing them to God. By doing so, they can come to live in this world, the world of a new heart, where God is the King of all kings; a heart where Queen Christian

Nature can, through Patience, fill every nook and cranny of it by the Holy Spirit and with the beauty of Christian Nature. A heart where the God-given wisdom of the experience of Time will come alongside of each new heart and teach what only Time, through God's wisdom, can teach."

So you see, my dear reader, may I now introduce you to the one who will become known as the famed "Saint Nicholaus!" All of the wealth he had accumulated before, he gave it all to God, who now gives it back to him, blesses it, and tells him to freely give it away to others to show them how much God loves them. Nicholaus comes to understand that the true value of money and physical possessions is not found in having it personally, but is found in how it is used to help others. God has impressed upon Nicholaus's heart the importance of defining his life, not by what he has, but by what he can freely give away.

As Nicholaus prepares to go to the other world, Time says, "Nicholaus, that's a big world, how will you travel about? It could be difficult with one person being able to give away gifts to all persons in such a big world." "God will provide a way," Nicholaus says. Queen Christian Nature says, "I have an idea, Nicholaus, to make this all possible. I have a deer friend who carried me on her back to God when I was little Evangeline. Permit me to call for her to come and bring her deer friends. I think they can help!" Then Christian Nature blows into the wind and the same ten foot tall female reindeer appears who had brought Evangeline to God. This enchanted reindeer calls for her deer friends and soon there are ten enchanted, flying reindeer, who dearly desire to be used by God to help Saint Nicholaus deliver God's gifts to others. "Ho! Ho! Ho! What a merry Christ-Day this is indeed," shouts Saint Nicholaus.

King Time then summons the citizens in the kingdom of God-created hearts and they present Nicholaus with an enchanted sleigh and harnesses for these deer saints. God Himself magically provides the power and an enchanted bag. "Ho! Ho! Ho! Merry Christ-Day," shouts Nicholaus, "for Jesus Christ, through the Holy Spirit, Time, and the Christian Nature-filled-saints has provided me with all I need to give gifts of happiness and joy to all, that they may clearly see God's love."

What a wonderful time of rejoicing this is indeed! Everyone in the kingdom of their God-created heart is being used by God to bring happiness and joy to others in a way that can only be seen with the eyes of one's own heart, in their imagination!

So, my dear reader, do you just smile at all this and say, "This is not real at all. It's only real in the heart of the imagination of this strange author!" Are you sure this is not real? Look into your own heart! Have there not been times when the Holy Spirit has lovingly whispered to you to actually do a particular thing, which only you can do, to help someone else, to be used by God to bring His love to others? Do you not realize that God may be using you to help someone else bring the gifts of God's love and joy to the heart of someone else through the loving hands of His saints?

Yes, my "deer" friend, you could be a flying deer in the sight of God, as you help in getting other saints to their destination! Maybe you helped to make the sleigh or the harnesses with your skillful hands. Not just anyone has that skill! Yes, indeed, my "deer" friend, Saint Nicholaus is real! His "deer ones" are real! His sleigh is real! They really do exist, now don't they? They exist in your God-created heart! In the world of your imagination! In the world that you bring from your heart and bring out through your mind, into this temporal world to be used by God to be a blessing to all those who seek to be a blessing to God!

So, my "deer" reader, does Saint Nicholaus exist? Do his "deer-ones" exist? Why don't you tell me! Could it be that you are Saint Nicholaus? Could it be that you are a "deer-one" helping him to deliver his dear gifts of love and joy to others?

This insignificant writer certainly does hope that you actually can prove your own existence in the heart of your imagination! The question is, in the form of what person do you actually exist? Are you Time, Christian Nature, Saint Nicholaus, or a deer-one?

As Saint Nicholaus loads his enchanted bag and prepares to fly with his deer-ones to the other world, Time and Christian Nature give him their special gifts. Time, gives the gift of time to Nicholaus so that he can find the time to bring God's gifts of joy and happiness to each and every person. Christian Nature gives the gift of Christian Nature to Nicholaus so that he can share Christian Nature to all who will give to God the gift of their heart. For in so doing, the Holy Spirit will fill their hearts with the beauty of Christian Nature. Queen Christian Nature also gives the ability to control nature for his benefit in the other world.

"Ho! Ho! Ho! Merry Christ-Day," cries Saint Nicholaus as he and his deer-ones disappear into the sky. They are off to take God's gifts of love, goodness, kindness, and God's grace to the hearts of those in the other world. "What a truly wonderful day of wholesome Christian fellowship this has been to all," Time says to Christian Nature, who then says, "Amen"!

Part Four

Life in the Enchanted Land

Chapter One

The God-Centered Nature Filled Heart

As the purity of a new, clean day fills the God-created lungs of each inhabitant in this enchanted land of the heart, it is as if not only the lungs, but also every organ in the body becomes like new again. A certain intoxication of freshness saturates every cell with the tantalizing excitement of the special treasure that is presented to each resident, as a gift to his or her God-enchanted hearts.

As we carefully study one resident, as he unwraps this gift that the day has given him, let's watch him with the eyes of our heart and see some of the treasures that the day gives to him. As the eyes of his heart focus on this gift, what he sees is amazing! A gentle, very soft rain kisses each creation of God with a delicate touch of its hands and lips, and seems to utter the words, "Good morning!" As our resident enjoys this special moment that he has learned by the wisdom taught him by the experience of Time, he has learned how to listen to the voice of the rain and enjoy its soothing melodies. Time has taught him how to diligently study it as it shares its life-enhancing benefits, and not just watch it and grumble over getting wet. As a student would diligently study his daily lesson, he has learned to see with his heart's eyes the beauty to be found in the simple puddles that form. He has come to experience the cool exhilarating excitement his heart feels as his face and hands are lovingly caressed with this divinely given treasure. His entire heart and soul, his entire being, is nurtured and soothed each morning with this life-enhancing balm from God Himself.

So you see, my friend, whereas, in the other world, where most seem to grumble, groan, and complain when they wake up to rain, and are prone to be negative from that moment on about all the other gifts that are given to them that day, it doesn't have to be that way. To those who choose to live in a God-created heart, which is filled with all the wonderment of what nature can bring, a simple rain can awaken one to God-given blessings.

As the rain departs the scene, another gift is freely given for all to enjoy. A beautiful rainbow welcomes all to its gifts of fresh colors, carefully and skillfully painted by the Master Artist to enrich the enjoyment of each day.

As we continue our investigation of this new day, we see magical drops of cherished sweetness gently falling from the trees, the flowers, the plants, and all objects of this enchanted land. They are there to enhance the lives of all. We see friendly swarms of honeybees constantly producing honey to provide the sweet taste of what only life can give to those who will partake of it. Unlike the selfish bees in the other world, who will seek to bring harm to you if you indulge yourself in the fruits of their labor, these honey bees freely give of themselves to enhance the happiness of all which their lives may touch. As a result of this, they never lack for anything and never die. What they constantly do to benefit others forever lives as a testimonial of their lives, and it seems as if the sweet memory of them never dies.

With the newness of each day, in our God-enchanted hearts, the assorted musicians assemble themselves in the kind branches of all providing trees, to fill the day with their unique talent of musical expertise, in order to enrich the heart and put a smile on the face of all. It is as if each colorful bird, in this orchestra of joy, has its own special instrument, that it shares its unique talent with that only it can provide, and the other birds cannot offer. When each one combines together, what a wonderful, enchanted orchestra is formed to bring true benefit and happiness into the lives of all.

Accompanying the natural musical vocal talent of the assorted feathered musicians, the singing rocks, with their friend, the melodious stream, wrap their loving arms around each other and seek to be a real blessing and source of encouragement to all who will simply listen with the ears of their heart.

Yes, indeed, my dear friend, each and every treasure that God has specially created in the world of nature, devotes itself to seeking to be a blessing and source of encouragement to all who will but look with the eyes of their heart. Each individual and distinct flower is designed to put a warm smile on your face. Each plant shares with you the gift that it produces for your happiness. Even the plants that don't produce an edible fruit or vegetable, if you will study it with the eyes of your heart, you will find that it produces its own unique beauty, in order to be a source of comfort and encouragement to all whom their lives may touch.

If each and every person will learn the skill of looking at all things with the eyes of the heart, listening to all things with the ears of the heart, and reaching out and touching all things with the hands of the heart, they will find the answer to a great mystery that some will never find. They will find that the real reason for life itself is not to live for themselves and for their own personal enjoyment. If they will but live to bring comfort, happiness, and enjoyment to all whom their lives may touch, they will have found the real meaning of life. They will have answered life's mystery, and they will be happy!

Chapter Two

The God-Centered Christian Nature Filled Heart

Oh what wonderful joy and happiness is to be found when one has truly given their heart to God! Oh what even more abundant joy is to be found when one lives in their God-created heart! When one begins to look at all things, listen to all things, and reach out and touch all things with the eyes, ears, and hands of one's own heart, great treasures are to be found. There is just so much beauty to be seen, heard, and felt if we will only make this our chosen place of habitation.

In our story, the King of all kings, God Himself, has appointed Time to be a sort of lesser king over God's dominion of the heart, and Christian Nature to be his queen. In this country, owned by God, each person seems to be under the influence of all they see, hear, and touch. From all of the beauty they see from the eyes of their heart in God's natural world, to all that their Holy Spirit, Christian Nature-filled eyes, ears, and hands show them in their Christian Nature-filled heart is truly amazing. Just as each object of nature seeks to point to its Creator, as if to give all glory to God, so does each citizen who lives here. Just as each object of nature seeks to be a real comfort and source of encouragement to all whom their lives may touch, so does each citizen who lives here.

It is as if all that they see, hear, and touch influences each citizen. Whether they are touched by the beauty of each other, or by the beauty of nature itself, they are filled with happiness and a desire to bring glory to God and be a blessing to everyone they come in contact with.

It is interesting to note, that we need to remember that nearly all persons who live in this enchanted God-created world of the heart, are actually still alive in the other world. Being still alive in the other world means they still have sinful human nature. As we will come to understand more fully in the next section, if we will allow the Holy Spirit to be the primary influence on our heart, the ravaging effects of our sinful human nature can be dramatically minimized. Such can be the impact upon all of us, if we will voluntarily choose to truly live in this enchanted God-created world in the imagination of our heart.

Let's see now how a typical cherished citizen lives in such a divinely magical land. As the eyes of his heart awaken each morning and intoxicate themselves with the beauty of nature, he is influenced to be a blessing to others, as others have blessed him. Just as he would partake of the nutritional delicious fruit of a tree, which only lives to point to God for its glory and to be a benefit to others, so he desires to do the same. As his life carefully and delicately comes in contact with another life, they each partake of each other's fruit off of their own tree of life. They are very careful to inspect each fruit on their own tree to be absolutely sure that it only contains wholesome, nutritious, and delicious fruit that it would bring glory to God and benefit to the citizen partaking of it. It would be a tragedy indeed, if there was a poison, worm-infested, sinful human-nature-consumed-fruit that others were eating off of their own supposed tree of life. Yes, my dear reader, if we were to allow our sinful human nature to be our primary influence, and not allow Christian Nature to be our primary influence, there would be no limit to the amount of poisonous toxin that would come from us and would be poisoning everyone who came into contact with our lives. Therefore, it is imperative that we carefully inspect our own fruit that comes from our heart each and every day!

So, as the citizens in this land come into contact with others each and every day, what kind of fruit is to be found upon each one? Everyone has friendly trees beckoning others to partake of their heart-enhancing, spiritual-health-promoting produce. Let's look at some of this fruit that has been patiently fed by both the hands of nature and by the beautiful hands of the Holy Spirit and Queen Christian Nature herself.

First, we see the fruit of a genuine "love." Not the kind of love if it will only receive love back; but a real unconditional love, like the kind we have personally experienced from our Savior, Jesus Christ. Oh yes, this fruit is so nourishing to the heart and brings real comfort to the hearts of all who partake of it.

There is also the fruit of "joy" coming from our tree of life, encouraging each one to partake of it as they journey through their adventure called "life." Because we are so regretfully human, it is so easy to become discouraged, depressed, sad, or just beaten down with all the discouraging moments that life hurls at us each day. How it so encourages us, though, to come alongside one who has their own tree filled with the fruit of joy. As they offer their fruit to us, the absolute magical taste of it so saturates our taste buds with a joyful happiness that it is as if we want to eat from this tree and stay close to it all the days of our lives. This tree understands that its only real purpose in life is to bring glory to God and be a source of comfort and encouragement to you.

There are also many citizens whose trees are filled with the fruit of "peace." These trees bring such a blessing of comfort to others who eat off of their tree of life. In the other world, it seems there is no peace. Whether in personal relationships, with the people they come in contact with, or between countries. It just seems as if so many are constantly instigating and looking to start wars with one another. So many want to partake of peace, but do not really reach forth to partake of the peace-fruit that is offered them, because their wicked and evil heart is rotted and stinks with pride! When our heart, from its "peace-tree" offers this fruit to others, it can be like a healing balm and accomplish the skill of being a softening agent on a hard heart. Is it any wonder why, in the enchanted land of a God-created heart, all are at peace with one another because they partake of this fruit off of each other's tree of life each day?

It appears, in this enchanted land, that no one is ever harsh because each one is constantly partaking of the fruit of "gentleness" off of the trees of others. Harshness, anger, and bitterness seem to define the lives of others so often in the other world. The craving to push others down through humiliation, rather than lifting others up through gentleness, seems to dominate the lives of those in the other world.

In the enchanted land of a God-created heart, very possibly the most prominent fruits to be found on the branches of these sumptuous trees are the fruits of "goodness" and "kindness." For you see, my dear reader, when our heart is constantly feeding on these fruits off of the trees of others, its influence in our heart causes it to bring forth the same fruit to feed others exactly the same wholesome food they need for that particular day. All of this for the purpose that God may be the One glorified and that He may use us to be a blessing to others!

The most wonderful tree of all, though, in this vast and wonderfully, divinely enchanted land of a God-created heart, is the tree of God's grace! Only one tree has this fruit, for only one tree can offer this fruit. That tree is the tree of God, the "Tree of God's Grace!" Just as in the warm, cozy feeling of a town square, where all of its citizens know each other and gather around to socialize, so this is a special place of gathering. Each one comes to enjoy each others company, share each others fruits, and just seek to do whatever possible to be a blessing to everyone they meet in this wonderful old-fashioned town square. For the ultimate enjoyment, all persons gather in the town square, where the massive Tree of God's Grace covers the whole square, with branches bursting forth with the fruit of God's grace dropping for all to enjoy. No one goes without partaking from this grace-tree of God everyday. What a wonderful time indeed! What a wonderful meal this day has brought to all.

Oh how happy everyone is each day as they partake of the Tree of God's Grace, a daily practice which everyone does in this land. Also, each day of partaking of the fruits of each person's fruit tree enriches the hearts of the citizens of this enchanted land. The fruits of love, joy, peace, gentleness, goodness, kindness and so many others, provides each saint with just what their bodies need for a healthy life. It seems the more fruit the citizens freely give to others, the more of the same fruit grows on their own trees to freely give to others. Then, just sitting on the comfortable benches, beckoning you to use them, and enjoying the fellowship of one with another, is an amazing sight to see. A sight, which can only be seen, when one chooses to look with the eyes of one's heart!

How could this not be the kind of world you would like to live in? "Just my imagination, not really real," you may say. It is real; it exists every day! However, it can only be seen, heard, and felt in the God-created, Holy Spirit, Christian Nature-filled heart!

Chapter Three

The Royal Adventure of King Time and Queen Christian Nature

What do a lesser king and queen do when both, they themselves and all their subjects, voluntarily and with a willing heart, submit themselves to serve the one and only King of all kings? We will come to see that they serve a wonderful purpose indeed! It is always interesting to see how God chooses each one for a special purpose, and then uses each of us to fulfill that purpose so that He may be glorified in it, and that it may be used to bring great benefit to others.

    Such is the case with the original Evangeline and Nathanael Nobody. Evangeline was taken from her mother at a very young age, which brought much sorrow and loss to her and her mother. Taught at the feet of God, this figurative, allegorical Holy Spirit begins her new life by filling God's created world, through the beautiful Patience of Christian Nature, with a beauty that no external eye could ever comprehend. As Christians begin arriving into this God-created, Holy Spirit-filled heart, they find beauty everywhere. From their surroundings, to the people they meet; everything seems to be consumed with a magical, enchanted,

Christian Nature-touched beauty, which can only be seen with the eyes of "faith," as we see all things with the eyes of the heart. As the allegorical Holy Spirit continues her particular adventure, in the form of the beautiful Patience, she is brought to, we may say, her love, in the person of Nathanael Nobody.

Thus begins the adventure of Patience and Nathanael Nobody. Even though a Christian, through the influence of the cares, demands, and responsibilities of the other world, Nathanael hadn't really looked at anything with the eyes of his heart for a long time. The Patience of Christian Nature begins to woo him to herself by: first helping him to see the beauty in the external world of nature, and, second, showing him that, the purpose of all things in the world of nature is to bring glory to God, and to benefit all whom their lives may touch. As Nathanael receives a reawakened heart, he begins to look at all things with the eyes of his heart and, as a result, sees many wonderful things, which he had never seen before. As he is now totally in love with the beautiful Patience, who is known by all in the kingdom of the heart as "Queen Christian Nature," he sees this allegory of the Holy Spirit for the first time with the eyes of his heart. What a magical and enchanted time this was as Queen Christian Nature tells him how God will uniquely use him to bring glory to God and be of benefit to others. After being taught by God Himself, Nathanael becomes a new person as "Time." His purpose, now, is to go about, together with Christian Nature, and share God's wisdom that comes through the experiences of our past mistakes, that can only be taught by Time and mature, Holy Spirit, Christian Nature-filled saints, who only live to bring glory to God and benefit to all whom their lives may touch.

So now, in the God-created kingdom of the heart, Holy God has given King Time and Queen Christian Nature the royal honor of temporarily ruling in his stead. Their purpose is to encourage each person to stay focused on why they live. They are to encourage others to realize that all we do, think, and say should be consistently bringing glory to God and being of benefit to others. So what does a king and queen do each day, you may ask, in such an enchanted kingdom of the heart?

As each day starts, they are always the first to welcome each new citizen into this God-created world of the new heart of the new Christian.

They warmly welcome the new citizen, who has just started looking with the eyes of their heart and has asked Jesus Christ to be their personal Savior from sin. They introduce him to numerous other Christians in this kingdom of a God-created heart, and before long the new citizen begins nibbling on the various fruits growing on these citizens' trees and begins to prosper. As the citizens give him a grand tour of this wonderful God-created kingdom, in this new world of his heart's imagination, he is totally brought under the influence of others and begins to now look at all things with the eyes of his heart. He becomes like one with all the other citizens in this world, as they all see what is truly real. They come to understand that our external eyes, ears, and hands are only for temporal use. The eyes, ears, and hands of our heart are what are truly real!

After the welcoming in of new citizens into this world, our king and queen spend significant time with many citizens, one at a time, carefully inspecting their fruit trees for any sinful worms or poisonous toxins. For we must remember that each citizen still has a sinful human nature. The king and queen see the imperativeness of coming alongside of each one, loving them, nurturing them, sometimes convicting them, and helping them in only a way that Time and Christian Nature can.

You see, both Time and Christian Nature fully understand that a truly good leader will spend time, and lots of it, with the people they rule over. Just as a good pastor of a congregation will devote much time to being with his people on an individual basis, so they can visibly see his love for them each day, so it is with a king and queen. If a pastor, or a king and queen spend time with the people individually, they will be showing their love for the people and the people will love them in return!

King Time and Queen Christian Nature are never, ever, separated. Wherever they go, they are together. Always holding hands, Christian Nature constantly snuggling up next to Time's heart, as seemingly their two hearts beat as one. Time, so often wrapping his arms around her and embracing her with such an affection of love that not only benefited them, but also, much more importantly, influenced others to show love toward those whom they love dearly.

The entire daily scene was just one of constant Christian love being shown toward each other. Basically, the citizens followed the example of their king and queen. Just as the king and queen showed love to each other and to all they came in contact with, so the citizens did likewise. Just as the king and queen spent time with their citizens, so the citizens spent much time with each other and shared encouragement with all whom their lives touched. Each one sought to keep their fruit trees free from the poisonous worms of sinful human nature. Also, each one beckoned others to partake of their healthy fruit, while they partook of the healthy fruit of others. What a truly wonderful fellowship each one has: the privilege of enjoying each other in this God-created heart in the world of their imagination!

Some readers still may not believe this world is real. "Just the writer's imagination," they may think. I ask you, those who only choose to see with their external eyes, to pay attention the next time you are around a congregation of saints. For if you look closely you will see, though far from perfect citizens, citizens who really do live in the kingdom of a God-created heart. They are seeking to bring out of their hearts the fruits of Christian Nature and the experience taught them by Time. They are seeking to share these with all whom their lives may touch, so that God, alone, may be glorified and that others may be benefited.

Now as we continue with our king and queen, our two sweethearts, we see that each day gives them another privilege. As they have welcomed each new one here, come alongside of each one and taught them, so now a very special day comes for each one. Receiving a message from heaven, the king and queen come to certain citizens each day and share the wonderful news with them, that this day is the day that a special angel has come for them. This is the day that the citizens have been waiting for ever since first arriving in this kingdom of their God-created heart. The king and queen come gladly, rejoicing, to the citizen and tell him this is his day to make the eternal move from this God-created heart in the world of his imagination, into heaven itself! Just about the time one thinks that life can not get any better than this, it does! The only thing better than living in a God-created heart in the world of our imagination, is actually living in a God-created heaven in the world of eternity based upon the facts of what the Bible teaches to be true!

Many have tried to imagine what heaven will be like. Just as we know that heaven is real, because we see it with the eyes of this wonderful God-created heart, in the world of our imagination, could it not be that the magical enchanted land of this story is actually real, if we will only see it with the eyes of our heart? Yes, indeed, my dear friend, look with the eyes of your heart and you will see the king and queen, the citizen who is so honored, and all others in the kingdom of the heart, who are all filled with rejoicing as this saint is prepared to enter heaven itself. Words can never fully convey the sort of joy that fills this honored saint. The many friends made in this wonderful enchanted land personally escort him. The king and queen, themselves, are taking the time to spend with him and personally escort him to the divinely appointed angel. As King Time carefully places the citizen's hand in the divinely appointed angel's hand, the citizen and the angel depart through the sky and into heaven. All this done while each one lovingly sheds tears of joy and wave a very temporary "goodbye" to a truly beloved saint, who has lived a life out of their God-created heart to bring glory to God and be of a benefit to others.

Chapter Four

The Homecoming of Saint Nicholaus

"Saint Nicholaus is coming to town! Saint Nicholaus is coming to town!" joyously shouts a citizen in this enchanted land of endless joy. Yes, indeed, my dear friend, King Time, in private, and under extreme secrecy, even from Queen Christian Nature, had asked Nicholaus to come back at this time for a very important occasion that only the king and Nicholaus knew anything about. The people all knew he was coming, but only the king and Nicholaus knew why.

What a wonderful time of merriment this produced in the hearts of all. You may say that the God-created hearts of each citizen, in this enchanted land, seems to always be filled with merriment. But I suppose one could say that for this special day, at least, it went to an even higher level. Strange as it may sound, in honor of the homecoming of this saint, and to welcome him home, everyone began doing something that had never been done before in this enchanted land in the heart of his or her imagination. They started with decorating all the trees in this vast forest of life with many colors of bright lights. Under each tree they carefully placed straw. On top of the straw they placed personally hand-carved objects representing their Lord and Savior, Jesus Christ, along with Mary and Joseph. They knew what Mary and Joseph looked like because one of the shepherds, who came that wonderful night, still lived in this enchanted land and was able to give the features of Jesus, Mary, and Joseph in precise detail. Remember, like Ahira Naphtali, there were some who stayed in this enchanted land long after their contemporaries had gone to heaven, because God had a special work for them to do. Thus, the skilled craftsmen went to work hand-carving these objects to lovingly place under each tree.

Everyone had a specific thing to do on this upcoming special day of rejoicing. Some were busy writing greeting cards, which was quite an undertaking, for they wrote one to everyone! Some were wrapping gifts, which they made themselves out of love. Again this was quite an undertaking, for they had gifts for everyone!

A certain time each day was set aside for groups to be formed in all locations, and the groups would sing lovely songs of merriment about how much God loves each one of us and what our Savior did for us. They all realized that except for what Jesus Christ did for us, none of this would be possible!

Each and every word and action that came from each person had one singular purpose. That purpose was to bring glory to God and to be a real source of comfort and encouragement to everyone whom their lives may touch.

At this time a special excitement seemed to be reaching unprecedented heights. The king and queen were slowly strolling along together, arm-in-arm, with Patience lovingly cuddled up next to her love. As they were greeting each kind face with a loving smile and kind words, the queen came up with an idea, smiled, and gently whispered into the ears of the king. Then they both smiled. The queen gently blew a kiss into the sky and, as if by magic, something happened in this enchanted land of the heart that had never happened before. Pure white flakes of powdered snow began to fall and tenderly caress, with loving kisses, each face they touched. The queen proclaimed to all that this was their king and queen's special gift to them as an expression of their love for each and every one. The purpose of this wonderful gift of beauty was to express the love that their king and queen have for them. It magically touched all things with loving kisses of Christian warmth. It was a wonderful example of what life can be like if one would choose to live in this wonderful world of enchantment, in their God-created heart. It is interesting to point out, that in the other world, in most cases the falling of snow is generally accompanied with bitter cold. In this world, there was no cold at all, only warmness coming down from their king and queen, as they were tenderly embracing each one with the comforting blanket of warmth that only Christians can truly understand.

You've probably guessed by now, but it needs to be said, that this special day will go down in eternal history; it will be marked on the calendar to be celebrated each year as a genuine "Merry Christ Day". As Saint Nicholaus seeks to remind all of what Jesus Christ has done for us and made available to us, so may we never forget to remind others of the same, when we come into their presence.

Gentle snow falling, colorful trees shining, cards and gifts being exchanged, the adoration of Jesus being proclaimed, merry songs of Jesus' love being melodiously sung from the affections pouring forth from the heart; yes, my dear friends, what a truly magical time of rejoicing this is!

As the tender snow continues to come, all of a sudden everything else stops! What is happening? A silence permeates the air. Everyone quietly gathers near the king and queen. Something is happening that has never happened before and will never happen again. Everyone strains to get a look at this scene and no one says a word. Women are sobbing the eyes of their heart out with their hands over their faces. Men can no longer prevent tears from flowing freely down their cheeks. Husbands tenderly wrap their arms around their wives and share in their tears. For you see, my dear friends, they are all witnessing their dearly beloved king and queen experiencing one of the most tender moments that any couple can experience. Let's look in amongst the vast multitude of people and see what is happening.

The king is down on one knee, looking lovingly into the queen's ocean-blue eyes, and holding her hands in his. He struggles, stutters, and seems to be sweating great drops of blood intermixed with tears as he says these words to the love of his heart, "Oh my darling, my only heart's desire, my forever love. How I love you so dearly! My heart belongs to you! Oh my darling, will you – I mean will you please – uh, uh … O Patience, I love you so much! Will you please marry me and be my forever bride?"

A huge gasp is heard throughout the crowd. Every eye goes immediately to their queen's ocean-blue eyes, including the pleading eyes of the king. The queen says nothing as her soft, caring, loving eyes embrace the very soul of her love through the eyes of her heart. She then says, "O Nathanael, I have always loved you with every cell of my being. I would sit under our special tree and hope for this day to happen long before you even cared if you ever saw me. I would cry my eyes out because you never cared about seeing anything with the eyes of your heart. I cried because it seemed you would never give me a chance to show you the love I have always had for you, because you never wanted to look at anything with the eyes of your heart. I had nearly given up hope. I waited so long for you and you wouldn't even take the time to see me. Then God did all this, Nathanael! Here we are, totally by God's grace, king and queen in God's vast domain! Yes, my forever love, yes, my darling, yes, my tender Nathanael, I will marry you. I will be your forever bride! How I so love you! Our love for each other will never end!" With this she dropped to her knees, put each hand lovingly on each cheek of Nathanael's crying face, and as nose touched nose, and their eyes looked intently into each other's, an amazing thing happened. Nathanael carefully planted a very passionate kiss on the honey-anointed lips of his sweetheart that lasted, seemingly, forever. Upon releasing his lips from hers, she immediately put her hands on both sides of his head, pulled his face to her sweet lips and fastened them there with an affectionate kiss that eyewitnesses say really did seem eternal!

Upon standing again, both were totally blushing as they held hands and temporarily looked down at their feet before hugging each other to the exuberant clapping of the people. It was at this moment that Aeromore comes forward with something hanging from his beak. That's right, an engagement ring! Not gaudy, but a pure diamond ring which Nathanael placed on Patience's finger and sealed with, that's right, yet another kiss. It was at this time that Patience began jumping up and down, patting her hands together, and shouting, "Let's all celebrate!" Ahira Naphtali cries out, "Bring out the flutes, the tambourines, and the mandolins. Let's all celebrate with our king and queen!"

All of a sudden, out of nowhere, comes Saint Nicholaus with his sleigh full of gifts of goodness, kindness, joy, and many others to share with the people. As Saint Nicholaus arrives with his deer-ones he says, "Ho! Ho! Ho! Merry Christ-Day everyone." He then looks around at all these people who have extremely happy looks on their faces and says, "Am I interrupting something here? Did I miss something?" Everyone breaks out into laughter in this joyous land that can only be imagined and seen clearly when one chooses to look with the eyes of one's heart!

Chapter Five

The Royal Wedding

Now Nicholaus, besides Patience, is Nathanael's best friend, and it is because Nathanael had sent a secret message to Nicholaus that he had come back for this special time. Hence, Nicholaus, with a smile reaching across his face, this roly-poly little bundle of happiness, cries out, "Ho! Ho! Ho! Merry Christ-Day everyone!"

Each and every person is filled with joy and happiness over all that has taken place in this enchanted land in the heart of their imaginations. After spending time with the people, Nathanael, holding Patience's hand, and along with Nicholaus, get alone with each other. For the king has a favor he wants to ask of Nicholaus. The king says, "Nicholaus, my friend, would you please do me the honor of being my best man at Patience's and my wedding?" Nicholaus, filled with joy, drops to one knee bows his head, and in the presence of his king and queen says, "I would consider it an honor to be the best man at the wedding of my two best friends." As these three saints enjoy sweet fellowship with one another, King Time asks Nicholaus, "So how goes it in the other world? What kind of reception have you received from those who live in the world of a different heart than the heart in which we live?"

"Well, my king and queen, for starters, they don't even believe that I exist! They have convinced themselves, in the world of their imagination, that Saint Nicholaus is just a figment of someone else's imagination! The only ones who believe I am real are very young children who look by faith, believing with the eyes of their young hearts. They are the only ones who see me clearly. They are a real source of joy to me. Everyone else, though, has convinced himself, or herself, that reality is only what they can see, hear, and touch with their temporal eyes, ears, and hands. It's really strange, my king and queen, for they have allowed the cares, demands, and responsibilities of that other world to so beat them down and consume all of their attention, that they no longer choose to see anything with the eyes of their heart."

Queen Christian Nature then says, while she holds King Time's hand and looks into his eyes, "It seems I once knew a man like that; a man who had to be lovingly shown how to look at all things with the eyes of his heart. Once he did, he became a new person, and my soon to be husband." To this the king gently kissed the queen, and Nicholaus smiled at both of them. Nicholaus goes on to say, "Not only this, my king and queen, but they don't even believe that King Time or Queen Christian Nature exist either!" "What?" shouts King Time. With a hand now on each of her cheeks, Queen Christian Nature lets out a gasp and cries out, "How can this be? How can anyone actually believe that we don't exist? We are real!" With this she stamps a foot to the ground and immediately all of the enchanted land feels a tremble.

"How can this be?" says the king to Nicholaus. "I really don't know," says Nicholaus to the king. Nicholaus continues, "There are so many wonderful things that these people could see in the heart of their imagination, that could bring glory to God, benefit to others, and happiness to themselves, if they would only look with the eyes of faith, with the eyes of their heart, to Jesus Christ as their Savior from their sins, and come and live with us in this God-created heart in the world of their imagination."

King Time then says, "It is strange indeed. They say reality is only what their external eyes, ears, and hands can see, hear, and touch, and yet, they all live in the world of their own imaginations too. It seems we all have our work cut out for us in seeking to convince these people of the difference between the permanent, what is real, and the temporary, what most seem to consider to be reality!" With this the king and queen once again hold hands, smile at Nicholaus, and say together, "We believe you are real Saint Nicholaus!"

As these three friends, once again, enjoy the merriment of one another's fellowship, Ahira Naphtali comes and gives a wink of the eye to King Time, who smiles and winks back. Queen Christian Nature notices the winks, smiles and says, "Alright you two, what's going on here?" The king tells her, "Ahira and Nicholaus will go with you, my love, to visit with the people today, for I have a special adventure to go on. But I'll return shortly." The queen, looking perplexed, now gets teary eyed and says, "Please don't leave me, my love. I know that I just can't live without you being by my side!" "I promise to return soon my love," says the king as he kisses her, waves, and disappears into the future. As Ahira and Nicholaus each take hold of a trembling hand of the queen, they take her to visit with the people, which helps relieve her anxiety.

Now to King Time: King Time had requested a private visit with God that only Ahira Naphtali, Nicholaus, and King Time knew of. The purpose was to get permission from God to go to heaven, find Patience's mother Eve, and bring her back so she could surprise her daughter and be her matron of honor at the king and queen's wedding. "Such a splendid idea," said Ahira and Nicholaus. "We'll distract the queen while you go on this adventure, God willing." The queen knew absolutely nothing about this. God approves of this adventure for King Time, who has the power to go anywhere he wants in the past, present, or future, but humbly seeks the approval of God. God reminds him, though, not to linger in heaven, and gaze and gawk at its splendor. Time realizes that Eve has already been told. So he is to go to heaven, get Eve, who is ecstatic with joy, and is eagerly waiting for him, and immediately bring her to meet her daughter with no delay. So the moment came when Time arrived in heaven, which stuns him so much with amazement that he falls backward on heavenly ground. Yes, he is in heaven! The splendor of the beauty of heaven is astonishing! But what he sees next is even more astonishing than the beauty of heaven. For you see, my dear friend, what King Time sees next causes him to rub his eyes with wonder. As he continues to be stunned, he falls back, once again, to the ground. Eagerly waiting for her soon-to-be son-in-law is Evangeline's mother, Eve. An absolutely perfect twin of her daughter! Absolutely amazing! As Nathanael stares, then gets up and slowly walks around and around her, carefully studying her every inch, he says nothing and then closely looks into her eyes. Her deep ocean-blue-water eyes are skillfully placed within a pure milky white face of complete beauty. Her thick, rich auburn hair is parted down the middle and cascades down to her waist. Behind her beautiful hair, this six foot tall masterpiece of creation was sobbing great tears of joy. The first words Nathanael heard from Eve, the mother of Evangeline, the love of Nathanael's heart was, "Do you find me pleasing to your sight, Nathanael? Please, I beg of you, please take me to my little Evangeline, who has always been the love of my heart. For only you, Nathanael, have the power and authority to take me to her."

Nathanael is in an absolute state of shock; still amazed at the person he is looking at; and still struggling to find the right words to say after being so astonished at seeing the exact replica of his beloved Patience. Eve and her daughter look exactly alike, in much the same way as one would look at oneself in a mirror. There is absolutely no difference at all! "How is this possible?" Nathanael says. He had always thought that no one could possess such ocean-blue-water eyes as Patience, but her mother does! As Patience, in age gives the appearance of a woman in her twenties so does her mother Eve! This is the very first woman who ever lived in the history of humanity. "How can this be?" thought Nathanael. Still stunned and unable to speak, Nathanael hears Eve say, "Yes, I know, we are a physical copy of each other. Please, let's go Nathanael, I want to be with my daughter." With this she places her hand in his, and Nathanael, still not knowing what to say, causes them to disappear from heaven together and reappear in the enchanted land of the heart.

What an amazing scene is about to take place. As they arrive, Ahira and Nicholaus immediately see their king with Eve. Nicholaus is also astonished and amazed. The queen is in conversation with some of the people and has her back turned toward Nathanael and Eve. An extremely large crowd is rapidly forming for they can now see their queen's mother and, they too, are absolutely amazed by their resemblance. The queen is wondering what has caused such a change in the people, who are now crying and sobbing great tears of joy. You see, everyone knew the story of Patience, which had become a famous part of history in this enchanted land.

The king, and Nicholaus have both withdrawn themselves now and are watching from a distance. Eve quietly stands about twenty feet behind her daughter. As Patience appears bewildered, Ahira Naphtali tells her, "Our king has brought you a special wedding gift. Would you like to see your wedding gift from our king?" Patience is filled with excitement and tells Ahira, "Yes, Ahira! Please show me!" He points to her to turn around and look. As she does her eyes meet her mother's deep ocean-blue-water eyes and what happens next is magical. Patience starts crying out, "Mama! Mama! Mama!" as they both run to each other and embrace, as only a mother and daughter can. The scene is wrought with great emotion. Such tender, delicate emotion of love between a mother and daughter has only been surpassed by the love of the king and the queen for each other. It was at this time that Ahira, the king and Nicholaus emerged. Patience and Eve now decided to see if Nathanael could recognize which one was his queen. As they stood side-by-side, they looked at the crowd and Ahira said, "My king we can't tell which one is our queen." Everyone said likewise, for no one could tell the difference. Ahira then said, "Our king, please show us which one is our queen, for it is impossible for us to tell." As Eve and Patience just stood side-by-side, both with identical smiles on their faces and looking at Nathanael with their identical ocean-blue eyes, Nicholaus whispers into Nathanael's ears, "Truly my king, I can't tell the difference. With God as my witness, I certainly cannot tell the difference!"

With all eyes now on the king, he immediately walks right up to his queen, and with no hesitation plants a very affectionate kiss on the lips of his love, wraps his loving arms around her and then announces to all that this is his sweetheart, the love of his heart and their queen. He says that he would know her if a thousand of her likenesses stood here. "How is that?" everyone asks. "My heart and Patience's heart beat together as one. All I needed to do was listen to the voice of our heart, the voice of my love speaking to me," the king says to all. To this the queen places a big kiss on the king's lips and says, "It would be absolutely impossible for anyone to love anyone as much as I love you!!!" Everyone, upon hearing this, erupts with applause and tears of joy freely flow from all eyes, for everyone loves their beloved king and queen dearly.

No love story such as this could ever be complete without the actual wedding of the two sweethearts, Nathanael and Patience. So, please give me the privilege of painting the picture for you in the heart of your imagination, of what this truly magical day was like. Everyone in this enchanted land came from far and wide. Everyone buzz ed with excitement as they seated themselves in this vast forest of life, in the sanctuary of Christian Nature's own choosing. The scene was already perfect, with the trees uniquely dressed in their bright lights and the warm snow gently covering everything with the soft blanket of Christian love. In addition to the gifts that everyone had given to each other, Nicholaus had personally given each person, yet, another personalized gift.

It would be very difficult for anyone not to want to live in a God-created world such as this. Everything about it is so wonderful and yet so real to everyone who has a heart to see it in the world of their imagination.

As the last person arrives, there is one more to come, Holy God, Himself. He has arrived to perform the marriage ceremony! As He proceeds up to front and center, no one sees the face of God for the Shekinah Glory of God conceals His face. As the song, "My Heart Is Filled with Thankfulness," is mysteriously sung by all and harmonizes wonderfully with Christian Nature, Eve slowly comes down the aisle and stands next to Nicholaus. The best man and the matron of honor are the official witnesses. Then, as the queen slowly walks down the aisle, all stand to see this model of purity, enriched in every detail by her natural beauty. As she approaches the altar, her mother places her daughter's hand in the hand of Nathanael, thus putting them together. She kisses both of them before stepping back to where Nicholaus is standing.

God then performs this divinely enchanted ceremony between Nathanael Nobody and Evangeline. The vows are exchanged that Nobody will never be separated from the beautiful Patience of Christian Nature, who both choose to live in the God-created heart in their own imaginations. At the conclusion of the ceremony, after everyone has departed to their own homes, Nicholaus and Eve go for a walk so that the king and queen can have some time alone.

As the king and queen walk together, holding hands for the first time as husband and wife, Nathanael blushes and asks Patience if she can have babies. With her head down, she says, "No," she can't have babies. She then raises her head, and with a smile that covers her face, her deep ocean-blue-water eyes look into his multi-colored eyes and she says, "But we can! We can have babies!" My dear friend, they do have babies, the most renown and famous babies ever in the Christian world. However, that story is beyond the scope of this one. That is in the next story to come. So my very special friend, is this the end? Or could it just be the beginning?

Conclusion

Do you remember when you first trusted Jesus Christ as your personal Savior from sin? Do you remember how it happened? How did you know that Jesus Christ was real? Did you actually see Him with your external eyes? I'm sure you would say that you saw him with the eyes of your heart. Some would call this the "eyes of faith." How did you hear God speaking to you? Did God actually, verbally, speak to your external ears? I'm sure you would say that you heard the Holy Spirit loving your heart to God, a sort of "wooing" of your heart to God. How did you reach out and touch Jesus Christ and ask Him to be your personal Savior from sin? Did you reach out and touch Him with your external hands? I'm sure you would say that you reached out and touched him with the hands of your heart, by faith.

My dear reader, do you see the point? We know that the Bible teaches us that our external eyes, ears, and hands are only temporary. We know that the Bible teaches us that the things, which are not seen by our external eyes, are real and are eternal. Some would say that when we look with the eyes of our heart by faith, when we hear with the ears of our heart by faith, and when we reach out and touch God by the hands of our heart by faith, we are just living in the world of our heart's imagination.

My brothers and sisters in Christ, no, it is certainly not our imagination at all! It is our faith in Jesus Christ of what we know to be true that comes from our heart. True reality can only come from our heart!

A real concern for this author is, what has happened to Christians today? We have gotten away from our place of beginning! Whereas, when we got "saved," we looked to God by faith in our heart, for we knew what was truly real was to be found by looking at all things with the eyes of our heart, by faith. Something awful has now happened though! Over time, like most people, some Christians only consider the temporary things they see, hear, and feel with their external eyes, ears, and hands to be "real." For someone to tell him or her, now, that reality can only be found in the world of his or her heart, is considered foolishness! It is to be seen as nothing more than one's imagination, fantasy, a person who should be put in a closet somewhere with the door locked so he can't get out and bring shame to his family! We say we believe God by faith and look to God only with the eyes, hear Him with the ears, and touch him with the hands of the heart, but technically that is a lie, for that is not the "real" world of reality for most Christians! Their real world of reality, if they are honest with themselves, consists of only that which they can see, hear, and touch with their external eyes, ears, and hands.

Very strange indeed! Most say that only externals are real. Yet all persons live in the reality they make for themselves in the heart of their own imaginations. To imagine and live in the world of faith and trust in Jesus Christ, looking at all things with the eyes of a redeemed heart, is living in the world of our imagination solely based on the facts of what Jesus Christ has done for us. True Reality! This is the world this author chooses to live in, and I only hope you will choose to join me.

To imagine, and live in, a world where there is no Jesus Christ would be to live in a world where the eyes of one's heart sees only pride, greed, vanity, lust, and all sorts of evil speaking. For this is what is real to them in the world of the heart of their imagination!

So, my dear reader, this is a call for Christians to come back and make their own personal choice to live in their redeemed heart, in the world of their imagination based upon the facts of what Jesus Christ has done for us. Choose to live in a world where the beautiful Patience of Christian Nature (the allegory of the Holy Spirit), seeks to fill every nook and cranny of your heart with the beauty of Christian Nature.

Remember how this story started? Remember that Nathanael Nobody, a Christian, had gotten away from looking at things with the eyes of his heart. At that time, he was only looking at all things with the eyes in his head. The Holy Spirit, through beautiful Patience, was seeking to lovingly woo him by helping him to go back to his roots and starts to help him see all things with the eyes of his heart. First, Patience helps him see, with his external eyes, the real purpose of all things in the world of Nature. He sees a purpose in all things, a beauty which he had never seen before. As the beautiful Patience of the Holy Spirit then gives him a newly awakened heart, he once again starts to look at all things with the eyes of his heart. He sees so many things, which he never thought possible. It's like he becomes a totally new person! He cries out for God to send someone to help him see clearly with the eyes of his heart. With this the beautiful Patience of Christian Nature (the Holy Spirit), shows her undying love for this saint, and promises to never leave him. Soon, Nathanael finds himself in a new world, a world that is real in the heart of his imagination. He sees people in this God-created heart who have been here for a long time, waiting for him to finally get here. Most importantly, he sees the allegory of the Holy Spirit, the beautiful Patience of Christian Nature, who has personally loved, guided, taught, and influenced him to look at all things with the eyes of his heart, for this is where true reality is found.

He finds himself becoming a new person, with a new identity, and a new purpose for being alive. His purpose, now and forever more, is not to live any longer for himself, but to live for the glory of God and to be of a benefit to others. After the Holy Spirit takes him into the very presence of God, where he is reawakened to truths he already knows, he goes forth with the love of his heart, Christian Nature. She fills his heart with what only Christian Nature can, and the two of them, together, go on adventures to live for the common purpose of bringing glory to God and being of a benefit to others.

Just as the Holy Spirit, through the beautiful Patience of Christian Nature, never leaves and never stops loving the Christian (who chooses to truly live in their God-created heart in the world of their 'real' imagination), so the Holy Spirit will never leave you either, but will affectionately love you, caress you, kiss you, and hug you in such a personal way that only a Christian who chooses to live in such a heart can understand.

So, my very dear friends, my cherished literary acquaintances, are we one with each other? In the introduction I invited you to come and live in this world of Nathanael Nobody and become him. For in reality, I believe that we are all, in a sense, Nathanael Nobody. We all must choose the world we wish to live in! This author has a deep passion for you to make, what I consider to be, the only wise choice for a Christian to make: to choose to live in a God-created heart in the world of your imagination. For this is actually not a world of our imagination, but a world of faith and trust, based upon the facts of what we know to be true about our Savior, Jesus Christ; where we see, hear, and feel all that is truly real with the eyes, ears, and hands of our heart!

I hope you have received great enjoyment from reading this story. If you have received even a portion of the enjoyment that it has brought me, then that would be wonderful. More importantly though, I hope and pray that the eyes of your newly awakened heart may now have been opened to the love of the Holy Spirit and God's amazing grace!

Your Forever Friend,
James A. Rousseau, Jr.
2017

www.ingramcontent.com/pod-product-compliance
Lightning Source LLC
Chambersburg PA
CBHW060400080526
44583CB00012B/404